FRONTIER COOKING

Publications International, Ltd.

Let's get social!

@Publications_International

@PublicationsInternational

www.pilcookbooks.com

TABLE of CONTENTS

BREAKFAST & BRUNCH

QUINOA AND OAT MUESLI

Makes 6¾ cups (about 12 servings)

1 cup uncooked quinoa

3 cups old-fashioned rolled oats

¼ cup unsweetened flaked coconut

¾ cup coarsely chopped almonds

½ teaspoon ground cinnamon

½ cup toasted wheat germ

¼ cup ground flaxseeds

1¼ cups dried fruit

1. Preheat oven to 350°F. Spread quinoa in single layer on baking sheet.

2. Bake 8 to 10 minutes until toasted and golden brown, stirring frequently. (Quinoa will make a slight popping sound when almost done.) Transfer to small bowl; cool completely.

3. Combine oats, coconut, almonds and cinnamon in large bowl. Spread in even layer on same baking sheet. Bake 15 minutes or until mixture is toasted and fragrant. Cool completely.

4. Combine cooled quinoa and oat mixture in large bowl; stir in wheat germ, flaxseeds and dried fruit.

Ham and Cheese Bread Pudding

Makes 8 servings

1 small loaf (8 ounces) sourdough, country French or Italian bread, sliced

3 tablespoons butter, softened

8 ounces ham or smoked ham, cubed

1 cup (4 ounces) shredded Cheddar cheese

3 eggs

2 cups milk

1 teaspoon ground mustard

½ teaspoon salt

⅛ teaspoon white pepper

1. Spray 11×7-inch baking dish with nonstick cooking spray. Spread one side of each bread slice with butter. Cut into 1-inch cubes; place on bottom of prepared dish. Top with ham; sprinkle with cheese.

2. Beat eggs in medium bowl. Whisk in milk, mustard, salt and pepper until blended. Pour egg mixture evenly over bread mixture; cover and refrigerate at least 6 hours or overnight.

3. Preheat oven to 350°F. Bake bread pudding, uncovered, 45 to 50 minutes or until puffed and golden brown and knife inserted into center comes out clean. Serve immediately.

BERRY BUCKWHEAT SCONES

Makes 8 scones

1¼ cups all-purpose flour

¾ cup buckwheat flour, plus additional for dusting

¼ cup packed brown sugar

1 tablespoon baking powder

½ teaspoon salt

½ cup (1 stick) cold butter, cubed

¾ cup fresh raspberries

¾ cup fresh blackberries

½ cup whipping cream

1 egg

1 tablespoon granulated sugar

Lemon curd or jam (optional)

1. Preheat oven to 375°F. Line baking sheet with parchment paper.

2. Combine all-purpose flour, ¾ cup buckwheat flour, brown sugar, baking powder and salt in food processor; pulse until combined. Add butter; pulse until pea-sized pieces of butter remain. Transfer mixture to large bowl; stir in berries.

3. Whisk cream and egg in small bowl; stir into flour mixture just until soft dough forms.

4. Gently pat dough into 8-inch round about ¾ inch thick on lightly floured surface. Cut into 8 wedges; arrange wedges 1½ inches apart on prepared baking sheet; sprinkle with granulated sugar.

5. Bake 20 to 25 minutes or until golden brown. Remove to wire rack to cool 10 minutes. Serve warm with lemon curd or jam, if desired.

Brunch Biscuit Bake

Makes 8 servings

8 ounces bacon, chopped

1 small onion, finely chopped

1 clove garlic, minced

¼ teaspoon red pepper flakes

5 eggs

¼ cup milk

½ cup (2 ounces) shredded white Cheddar cheese, divided

¼ teaspoon salt

⅛ teaspoon black pepper

1 package (16 ounces) refrigerated jumbo buttermilk biscuits (8 biscuits)

1. Preheat oven to 425°F. Cook bacon in large cast iron skillet until crisp. Remove to paper towel-lined plate. Drain and reserve drippings, leaving 1 tablespoon in skillet.

2. Add onion, garlic and red pepper flakes to skillet; cook and stir 8 minutes or until onion is softened. Set aside to cool slightly.

3. Whisk eggs, milk, ¼ cup cheese, salt and black pepper in medium bowl until well blended. Stir in onion mixture.

4. Wipe out any onion mixture remaining in skillet; grease with additional drippings, if necessary. Separate biscuits and arrange in single layer in bottom of skillet. (Bottom of skillet should be completely covered.) Pour egg mixture over biscuits; sprinkle with remaining ¼ cup cheese and cooked bacon.

5. Bake about 25 minutes or until puffed and golden brown. Serve warm.

Quick Jelly-Filled Biscuit Doughnuts

Makes 10 doughnuts

Vegetable oil for frying

1 can (about 7 ounces) refrigerated biscuits (10 biscuits)

⅓ cup coarse sugar

1 cup strawberry preserves*

*If preserves are very chunky, process in food processor 10 seconds or press through fine-mesh sieve.

1. Pour about 2 inches of oil into Dutch oven or large heavy saucepan; clip deep-fry or candy thermometer to side of pot. Heat over medium-high heat to 360° to 370°F. Line large wire rack with paper towels.

2. Separate biscuits. Place sugar in medium bowl. Fry biscuits in batches 1 minute per side or until puffed and golden. Remove to prepared wire rack. Immediately toss in sugar to coat.

3. Fit piping bag with medium star tip; fill bag with preserves. Poke hole in side of each doughnut with paring knife; fill with jam. Serve immediately.

Breakfast Migas

Makes 6 servings

1 tablespoon olive oil

1 small onion, chopped

1 jalapeño pepper,* seeded and diced

3 corn tortillas, cut into 1-inch pieces

1 medium tomato, halved, seeded and diced

6 eggs

2 tablespoons chunky salsa

1 cup (4 ounces) shredded Monterey Jack cheese

1 small ripe avocado, diced

1 tablespoon lime juice

Sour cream and fresh cilantro sprigs (optional)

Jalapeño peppers can sting and irritate the skin, so wear rubber gloves when handling peppers and do not touch your eyes.

1. Heat oil in large nonstick skillet over medium heat. Add onion and jalapeño; cook and stir 3 minutes or until vegetables are softened.

2. Add tortillas and tomato; cook about 2 minutes or until soft and heated through.

3. Lightly beat eggs and salsa in small bowl. Pour mixture into skillet; cook until eggs are firmly scrambled, stirring occasionally.

4. Remove skillet from heat; stir in cheese. Top with avocado tossed in lime juice, sour cream and cilantro.

Note: Migas, a Mexican breakfast dish, is traditionally made in a skillet with stale tortillas that are torn into small pieces by hand.

Cornmeal Pancakes

Makes 4 servings

2 cups buttermilk

2 eggs, lightly beaten

¼ cup sugar

2 tablespoons butter, melted

1½ cups yellow cornmeal

¾ cup all-purpose flour

1½ teaspoons baking powder

1 teaspoon salt

Fresh blueberries (optional)

Additional butter (optional)

1. Combine buttermilk, eggs, sugar and 2 tablespoons butter in large bowl; beat until well blended. Combine cornmeal, flour, baking powder and salt in medium bowl; stir into buttermilk mixture just until blended. Let stand 5 minutes.

2. Lightly grease griddle or large skillet; heat over medium heat. Pour batter onto griddle ⅓ cup at a time. Cook 3 minutes or until tops of pancakes are bubbly and appear dry; turn and cook 2 minutes or until bottoms are golden. Top with blueberries and additional butter, if desired.

Breakfast Sausage Monkey Muffins

Makes 12 muffins

12 ounces bulk pork sausage

1 egg, beaten

1½ cups (6 ounces) shredded Mexican cheese blend, divided

2 packages (about 7 ounces each) refrigerated buttermilk biscuits (10 biscuits per package)

1. Preheat oven to 350°F. Spray 12 standard (2½-inch) muffin cups with nonstick cooking spray.

2. Cook and stir sausage in large skillet over medium-high heat about 8 minutes or until no longer pink, breaking apart any large pieces. Spoon sausage and drippings into large bowl; let cool 2 minutes. Add egg; stir until blended. Stir in 1¼ cups cheese.

3. Separate biscuits; cut each biscuit into 4 pieces with scissors. Roll biscuit pieces in sausage mixture to coat; place 6 to 7 biscuit pieces in each muffin cup. Sprinkle with remaining ¼ cup cheese.

4. Bake about 22 minutes or until golden brown. Remove muffins to paper towel-lined plate. Serve warm.

BAKED PUMPKIN FRENCH TOAST

Makes 6 servings

1 tablespoon butter, softened

1 loaf challah or egg bread (12 to 16 ounces), cut into ¾-inch-thick slices

7 eggs

1¼ cups whole milk

⅔ cup canned pumpkin

1 teaspoon vanilla

½ teaspoon pumpkin pie spice

⅛ teaspoon salt

3 tablespoons sugar

2 teaspoons ground cinnamon

Maple syrup

1. Generously grease 13×9-inch baking dish with butter. Arrange bread slices in dish, fitting slices in tightly.

2. Combine eggs, milk, pumpkin, vanilla, pumpkin pie spice and salt in medium bowl; beat until well blended. Pour over bread in prepared baking dish; turn slices to coat completely. Cover and refrigerate 8 hours or overnight.

3. Preheat oven to 350°F. Combine sugar and cinnamon in small bowl; mix well. Turn bread slices again; sprinkle generously with cinnamon-sugar.

4. Bake about 30 minutes or until bread is puffy and golden brown. Serve immediately with maple syrup.

Chicken and Waffles with Spicy Maple Syrup

Makes 4 to 6 servings

Chicken

- ½ cup milk
- 1 egg
- 1¼ pounds chicken tenderloins (about 8 pieces)
- 1½ cups plain panko bread crumbs
- 1 teaspoon paprika
- 1 teaspoon garlic powder
- 1 teaspoon salt
- ½ teaspoon black pepper
- ¼ cup vegetable oil

Waffles

- 2 cups baking mix
- 1⅓ cups milk
- 1 egg

Spicy Maple Syrup

- ½ cup maple syrup
- 2 teaspoons sriracha hot sauce

1. Whisk ½ cup milk and 1 egg in medium bowl until blended. Add chicken; toss to coat.

2. Combine panko, paprika, garlic powder, salt and pepper in shallow dish or pie plate. Dip chicken, one piece at a time, in panko mixture to coat completely, pressing down lightly to adhere. Remove to plate.

3. Heat oil in large nonstick skillet over medium heat. Cook chicken 6 minutes per side or until golden brown and no longer pink in center. Remove to clean plate; tent with foil to keep warm.

4. Preheat classic waffle maker to medium; spray with nonstick cooking spray. Combine baking mix, 1⅓ cups milk and 1 egg in medium bowl until well blended. Pour ¾ cup batter into waffle maker; cook 3 to 4 minutes or until golden brown. Remove to serving plate. Repeat with remaining batter.

5. Combine maple syrup and hot sauce in small bowl; mix well. Top waffles with chicken; drizzle with syrup.

Classic Cinnamon Buns

Makes 8 buns

Dough

- 1 teaspoon active dry yeast
- ½ cup warm milk (110°F)
- 1 egg, beaten
- ¼ cup granulated sugar
- 2 tablespoons butter, softened, plus additional for pan
- ½ teaspoon salt
- 2 cups all-purpose flour

Filling

- ½ cup packed brown sugar
- 1 tablespoon ground cinnamon
  Pinch salt
- 3 tablespoons butter, softened

Icing

- ¾ cup powdered sugar
- 2 ounces cream cheese, softened
- 2 tablespoons butter, softened
- ¼ teaspoon vanilla
  Pinch salt

1. Dissolve yeast in warm milk in large bowl of electric mixer. Add egg, granulated sugar, 2 tablespoons butter and ½ teaspoon salt; beat at medium speed until well blended. Add flour; beat at low speed until dough begins to come together. Knead dough with dough hook at low speed about 5 minutes or until smooth, elastic and slightly sticky.

2. Shape dough into a ball. Place in large greased bowl; turn to grease top. Cover and let rise in warm place about 1 hour or until doubled in size. Meanwhile, for filling, combine brown sugar, cinnamon and pinch of salt in small bowl; mix well.

3. Grease large cast iron skillet generously with butter. Roll out dough into 12×8-inch rectangle on floured surface. Spread 3 tablespoons butter evenly over dough; top with cinnamon-sugar mixture. Beginning with long side, roll up dough tightly jelly-roll style; pinch seam to seal. Cut log crosswise into

8 slices; place slices cut sides up in prepared skillet. Cover and let rise in warm place about 30 minutes or until almost doubled in size. Preheat oven to 350°F.

4. Bake 20 to 25 minutes or until golden brown. Meanwhile, for icing, combine powdered sugar, cream cheese, 2 tablespoons butter, vanilla and pinch of salt in medium bowl; beat with electric mixer at medium speed 2 minutes or until smooth and creamy. Spread icing generously over warm cinnamon buns.

Mini Spinach Frittatas

Makes 12 mini frittatas (4 to 6 servings)

1 tablespoon olive oil

½ cup chopped onion

8 eggs

¼ cup plain yogurt

1 package (10 ounces) frozen chopped spinach, thawed and squeezed dry

½ cup (2 ounces) shredded white Cheddar cheese

¼ cup grated Parmesan cheese

¾ teaspoon salt

⅛ teaspoon black pepper

⅛ teaspoon ground red pepper

Dash ground nutmeg

1. Preheat oven to 350°F. Spray 12 standard (2½-inch) muffin cups with nonstick cooking spray.

2. Heat oil in large nonstick skillet over medium heat. Add onion; cook and stir about 5 minutes or until tender. Set aside to cool slightly.

3. Whisk eggs and yogurt in large bowl. Stir in spinach, Cheddar, Parmesan, salt, black pepper, red pepper, nutmeg and onion until blended. Divide mixture evenly among prepared muffin cups.

4. Bake 20 to 25 minutes or until eggs are puffed and firm and no longer shiny. Cool in pan 2 minutes. Loosen bottom and sides with small spatula or knife; remove to wire rack. Serve warm, cold or at room temperature.

Baked Apple Pancake

Makes 2 to 4 servings

3 tablespoons butter

3 medium Granny Smith apples (about 1¼ pounds), peeled and cut into ¼-inch slices

½ cup packed dark brown sugar

1½ teaspoons ground cinnamon

½ teaspoon plus pinch salt, divided

4 eggs

⅓ cup whipping cream

⅓ cup milk

2 tablespoons granulated sugar

½ teaspoon vanilla

⅔ cup all-purpose flour

1. Melt butter in 8-inch ovenproof nonstick or cast iron skillet over medium heat. Add apples, brown sugar, cinnamon and pinch of salt; cook about 8 minutes or until apples begin to soften, stirring occasionally. Spread apples in even layer in skillet; set aside to cool 30 minutes.

2. After apples have cooled 30 minutes, preheat oven to 425°F. Whisk eggs in large bowl until foamy. Add cream, milk, granulated sugar, vanilla and remaining ½ teaspoon salt; whisk until blended. Sift flour into egg mixture; whisk until batter is well blended and smooth. Set aside 15 minutes.

3. Stir batter; pour evenly over apple mixture. Place skillet on rimmed baking sheet in case of drips (or place baking sheet or piece of foil in oven beneath skillet).

4. Bake about 16 minutes or until top is golden brown and pancake is loose around edge. Cool 1 minute; loosen edge of pancake with spatula, if necessary. Place large serving plate or cutting board on top of skillet and invert pancake onto plate. Serve warm.

HOMESTEAD BISCUITS AND GRAVY

Makes 8 servings

3 tablespoons canola or vegetable oil, divided

8 ounces bulk breakfast sausage

2¼ cups plus 3 tablespoons biscuit baking mix, divided

2⅔ cups whole milk, divided

¼ teaspoon salt

¼ teaspoon black pepper

1. Preheat oven to 450°F. Heat 1 tablespoon oil in large skillet over medium heat. Add sausage; cook 6 to 8 minutes or until browned, stirring to break up meat. Remove to plate with slotted spoon.

2. Add remaining 2 tablespoons oil to skillet. Add 3 tablespoons biscuit mix; whisk until smooth. Gradually add 2 cups milk; cook and stir 3 to 4 minutes or until mixture comes to a boil. Cook and stir 1 minute or until thickened. Add sausage; cook and stir 2 minutes. Season with salt and pepper.

3. Combine remaining 2¼ cups biscuit mix and ⅔ cup milk in medium bowl; stir until blended. Spoon batter into 8 mounds on gravy mixture.

4. Bake 8 to 10 minutes or until biscuits are golden brown. Serve warm with gravy.

Sugar and Spice Doughnuts

Makes 14 to 16 doughnuts

2¾ cups all-purpose flour, plus additional for work surface

¼ cup cornstarch

1 teaspoon salt

1 teaspoon baking powder

½ teaspoon baking soda

1½ teaspoons ground cinnamon, divided

½ teaspoon ground nutmeg

2 cups sugar, divided

2 eggs

¼ cup (½ stick) butter, melted

¼ cup applesauce

1 teaspoon vanilla

½ cup buttermilk

Vegetable oil for frying

1. Combine 2¾ cups flour, cornstarch, salt, baking powder, baking soda, ½ teaspoon cinnamon and nutmeg in large bowl; mix well.

2. Beat 1 cup sugar and eggs in large bowl with electric mixer at high speed 3 minutes or until pale and thick. Beat in butter, applesauce and vanilla until blended. Add flour mixture alternately with buttermilk, beating at low speed after each addition. Press plastic wrap directly onto surface of dough; refrigerate at least 1 hour.

3. Pour about 2 inches oil into Dutch oven or large heavy saucepan; clip deep-fry or candy thermometer to side of pot. Heat over medium-high heat to 360° to 370°F.

4. Meanwhile, generously flour work surface. Turn out dough onto work surface; dust top with flour. Roll dough about ¼ inch thick; cut out doughnuts with floured doughnut cutter. Gather and reroll scraps. For topping, combine remaining 1 cup sugar and 1 teaspoon cinnamon in large bowl. Line large wire rack with paper towels.

5. Working in batches, add doughnuts to hot oil (do not crowd pan). Cook 1 minute per side or until golden brown, adjusting heat as necessary to maintain temperature during frying. Drain doughnuts briefly on prepared wire rack, then toss in cinnamon sugar to coat both sides. Cool on wire racks.

APPETIZERS & SNACKS

BUFFALO CHICKEN DIP

Makes 5 cups

2 packages (8 ounces each) cream cheese, softened and cut into pieces

1 jar (12 ounces) restaurant-style wing sauce

1 cup ranch dressing

2 cups shredded cooked chicken (from 1 pound boneless skinless chicken breasts)

2 cups (8 ounces) shredded Cheddar cheese

Tortilla chips

Celery sticks

1. Combine cream cheese, wing sauce and ranch dressing in large saucepan; cook over medium-low heat 7 to 10 minutes or until cream cheese is melted and mixture is smooth, whisking frequently.

2. Combine chicken and Cheddar in large bowl. Add cream cheese mixture; stir until well blended. Pour into serving bowl; serve warm with tortilla chips and celery sticks.

Pepperoni Bread

Makes about 6 servings

1 package (about 14 ounces) refrigerated pizza dough

8 slices provolone cheese

20 to 30 slices pepperoni (about half of 6-ounce package)

½ teaspoon Italian seasoning

¾ cup (3 ounces) shredded mozzarella cheese

½ cup grated Parmesan cheese

1 egg, beaten

Marinara sauce, heated

1. Preheat oven to 400°F. Unroll pizza dough on sheet of parchment paper with long side in front of you. Cut off corners of dough to create oval shape.

2. Arrange half of provolone slices over bottom half of oval, cutting to fit as necessary. Top with pepperoni; sprinkle with ¼ teaspoon Italian seasoning. Top with mozzarella, Parmesan and remaining provolone slices; sprinkle with remaining ¼ teaspoon Italian seasoning.

3. Fold top half of dough over filling to create half moon (calzone) shape; press edges with fork or pinch edges to seal. Transfer calzone with parchment paper to large baking sheet; curve slightly into crescent shape. Brush with beaten egg.

4. Bake about 16 minutes or until crust is golden brown. Remove to wire rack to cool slightly. Cut crosswise into slices; serve warm with marinara sauce.

Crunchy Parmesan Zucchini Sticks

Makes about 6 servings

3 medium zucchini

1 package (3 ounces) ramen noodles, any flavor

½ cup shredded Parmesan cheese

½ cup all-purpose flour

1 egg

1 tablespoon water

Prepared marinara sauce for dipping

1. Preheat oven to 400°F. Line baking sheet with parchment paper. Cut zucchini in half crosswise, then cut each half into four sticks.

2. Combine noodles and cheese in food processor or blender; pulse until fine crumbs form. Pour into shallow dish.

3. Combine flour and ramen seasoning packet in another shallow dish; stir to combine. Whisk egg and water in third shallow dish.

4. Dip one zucchini stick first in flour, then in egg mixture, shaking off excess. Roll in noodle mixture to coat. Place on prepared baking sheet. Repeat with remaining zucchini.

5. Bake 20 minutes or until zucchini is softened and coating is golden brown. Serve warm with marinara sauce for dipping.

Sweet Hot Chicken Wings

Makes about 36 appetizers

3 pounds chicken wings

¾ cup salsa

⅔ cup honey

⅓ cup soy sauce

¼ cup Dijon mustard

2 tablespoons vegetable oil

1 tablespoon grated fresh ginger

½ teaspoon grated orange peel

½ teaspoon grated lemon peel

Ranch dressing (optional)

1. Cut off and discard wing tips from chicken. Cut each wing in half at joint. Place wings in 13×9-inch baking dish.

2. Combine salsa, honey, soy sauce, mustard, oil, ginger, orange peel and lemon peel in small bowl; mix well. Pour over wings; toss to coat. Cover and marinate in refrigerator at least 6 hours or overnight.

3. Preheat oven to 400°F. Line rimmed baking sheet with foil. Place wings in single layer on prepared baking sheet. Pour marinade over wings.

4. Bake 40 to 45 minutes until brown. Serve warm with ranch dressing, if desired.

Black Bean Salsa

Makes 6 servings

1 can (about 15 ounces) black beans, rinsed and drained

1 cup frozen corn, thawed

1 tomato, chopped

¼ cup chopped green onions

2 tablespoons chopped fresh cilantro

2 tablespoons lemon juice

1 tablespoon vegetable oil

1 teaspoon chili powder

¼ teaspoon salt

6 corn tortillas

Lime wedges and additional fresh cilantro (optional)

1. Combine beans, corn, tomato, green onions, cilantro, lemon juice, oil, chili powder and salt in medium bowl; mix well.

2. Preheat oven to 400°F. Cut each tortilla into eight wedges; place on ungreased baking sheet.

3. Bake 6 to 8 minutes or until edges begin to brown; cool slightly. Serve tortilla wedges with salsa. Garnish with lime wedges and cilantro.

Note: This salsa can also be served as a side dish with chicken or fish, on top of a mixed green salad, or wrapped in a tortilla.

Corn Fritters

Makes 6 to 8 servings

½ cup all-purpose flour

1 teaspoon sugar

½ teaspoon baking powder

½ teaspoon salt

⅛ teaspoon dried thyme

Pinch ground red pepper (optional)

1 egg

¼ cup half-and-half or milk

1 cup cooked corn kernels from 1 large ear *or* 1 cup frozen corn, thawed

Vegetable oil

Chunky mild salsa or marinara sauce

1. Combine flour, sugar, baking powder, salt, thyme and red pepper, if desired, in large bowl; mix well.

2. Beat egg and half-and-half in small bowl. Add to flour mixture; stir just until blended. Stir in corn.

3. Pour oil into large skillet to depth of ¼ inch. Heat over medium heat until drop of batter sizzles and turns golden in less than a minute. Drop batter by rounded tablespoonfuls into hot oil. Cook 3 minutes or until golden brown; turn and cook 1 minute or until golden brown.

4. Drain on paper towel-lined plate. Serve hot with salsa for dipping.

BBQ Chicken Flatbread

Makes 4 servings

3 tablespoons red wine vinegar

2 teaspoons sugar

¼ red onion, thinly sliced (about ⅓ cup)

3 cups shredded rotisserie chicken

½ cup barbecue sauce

1 package (about 14 ounces) refrigerated pizza dough

All-purpose flour, for dusting

1½ cups (6 ounces) shredded mozzarella cheese

1 green onion, thinly sliced

2 tablespoons chopped fresh cilantro

1. Preheat oven to 400°F; place rack in lower third of oven. Line baking sheet with parchment paper.

2. For pickled onion, combine vinegar and sugar in small bowl; stir until sugar is dissolved. Add red onion; cover and let stand at room temperature while preparing flatbread. Combine chicken and barbecue sauce in medium bowl; toss to coat.

3. Roll out dough into 11×9-inch rectangle on lightly floured surface. Transfer dough to prepared baking sheet; top with cheese and barbecue chicken mixture.

4. Bake about 12 minutes or until crust is golden brown and crisp and cheese is melted. Drain liquid from red onion; sprinkle over flatbread. Garnish with green onion and cilantro. Serve immediately.

Spinach-Artichoke Dip

Makes 6 to 8 servings

1 package (8 ounces) baby spinach

1 package (8 ounces) cream cheese, softened

¼ cup mayonnaise

1 clove garlic, minced

1 teaspoon dried basil

½ teaspoon dried thyme

¼ teaspoon salt

¼ teaspoon red pepper flakes

¼ teaspoon black pepper

1 can (about 14 ounces) artichoke hearts, drained and chopped

¾ cup grated Parmesan cheese, divided

Toasted French bread slices or tortilla chips

1. Preheat oven to 350°F. Spray 8-inch oval, round or square baking dish with nonstick cooking spray.

2. Place spinach in large microwavable bowl; cover and microwave on HIGH 2 minutes or until wilted. Uncover; let stand until cool enough to handle. Squeeze dry and coarsely chop.

3. Whisk cream cheese, mayonnaise, garlic, basil, thyme, salt, red pepper flakes and black pepper in medium bowl until well blended. Stir in spinach, artichokes and ½ cup Parmesan. Spread in prepared baking dish; sprinkle with remaining ¼ cup Parmesan.

4. Bake about 30 minutes or until edges are golden brown. Cool slightly; serve warm with toasted bread slices.

Pepperoni-Stuffed Mushrooms

Makes 4 to 6 servings

16 medium mushrooms

1 tablespoon olive oil

½ cup finely chopped onion

2 ounces pepperoni, finely chopped (about ½ cup)

¼ cup finely chopped green bell pepper

½ teaspoon seasoned salt

¼ teaspoon dried oregano

⅛ teaspoon black pepper

½ cup crushed buttery crackers (about 12)

¼ cup grated Parmesan cheese

1 tablespoon chopped fresh parsley, plus additional for garnish

1. Preheat oven to 350°F. Line baking sheet with foil; spray foil with nonstick cooking spray.

2. Clean mushrooms; remove stems and set aside caps. Finely chop stems.

3. Heat oil in large skillet over medium-high heat. Add onion; cook and stir 2 to 3 minutes or until softened. Add mushroom stems, pepperoni, bell pepper, seasoned salt, oregano and black pepper; cook and stir about 5 minutes or until vegetables are tender but not browned.

4. Remove from heat; stir in crushed crackers, cheese and 1 tablespoon parsley until blended. Spoon mixture into mushroom caps, mounding slightly in centers. Place filled caps on prepared baking sheet.

5. Bake about 20 minutes or until heated through. Garnish with additional parsley.

CRISPY RANCH CHICKEN BITES

Makes 4 servings

1 **pound boneless skinless chicken breasts**

¾ **cup ranch dressing, plus additional for serving**

2 **cups panko bread crumbs**

1. Preheat oven to 375°F. Line baking sheet with foil; spray foil with nonstick cooking spray.

2. Cut chicken into 1-inch cubes. Place ¾ cup ranch dressing in small bowl. Spread panko in shallow dish. Dip chicken in ranch dressing; shake off excess. Roll in panko to coat. Place breaded chicken on prepared baking sheet. Spray with cooking spray.

3. Bake 15 to 17 minutes or until golden brown and cooked through, turning once. Serve with additional ranch dressing.

Spicy Roasted Chickpeas

Makes 6 to 8 servings

1 can (about 15 ounces) chickpeas, rinsed and drained

3 tablespoons olive oil

½ teaspoon salt

½ teaspoon black pepper

¾ to 1 tablespoon chili powder

⅛ to ¼ teaspoon ground red pepper

1 lime, cut into wedges

1. Preheat oven to 400°F.

2. Combine chickpeas, oil, salt and black pepper in large bowl; toss to coat. Spread in single layer on 15×10-inch jelly-roll pan.

3. Bake 15 minutes or until chickpeas begin to brown, shaking pan twice.

4. Sprinkle with chili powder and red pepper. Bake 5 minutes or until dark golden-red. Serve with lime wedges.

POTATO SKINS

Makes 6 to 8 servings

8 medium baking potatoes (6 to 8 ounces each)

1 tablespoon vegetable oil

1 teaspoon salt

⅛ teaspoon black pepper

1 tablespoon butter, melted

1 cup (4 ounces) shredded Cheddar cheese

8 slices bacon, crisp-cooked and coarsely chopped

1 cup sour cream

3 tablespoons snipped fresh chives

1. Preheat oven to 400°F.

2. Prick potatoes all over with fork. Rub oil over potatoes; sprinkle with salt and pepper. Place in 13×9-inch baking pan. Bake 1 hour or until fork-tender. Let stand until cool enough to handle. *Reduce oven temperature to 350°F.*

3. Cut potatoes in half lengthwise; cut small slice off bottom of each half so potato halves lay flat. Scoop out soft middles of potato skins; reserve for another use. Place potato halves skin sides up in baking pan; brush potato skins with butter.

4. Bake 20 to 25 minutes or until crisp. Turn potatoes over; top with cheese and bacon. Bake 5 minutes or until cheese is melted. Cool slightly. Top with sour cream and chives just before serving.

Chicken Bacon Quesadillas

Makes 4 servings

4 teaspoons vegetable oil, divided

4 (8-inch) flour tortillas

1 cup (4 ounces) shredded Colby-Jack cheese

2 cups coarsely chopped cooked chicken

4 slices bacon, crisp-cooked and coarsely chopped

½ cup pico de gallo, plus additional for serving

Sour cream and guacamole (optional)

1. Heat large nonstick skillet over medium heat; brush with 1 teaspoon oil. Place one tortilla in skillet; sprinkle with ¼ cup cheese. Spread ½ cup chicken over one half of tortilla; top with one fourth of bacon and 2 tablespoons pico de gallo.

2. Cook 1 to 2 minutes or until cheese is melted and bottom of tortilla is lightly browned. Fold tortilla over filling, pressing with spatula. Transfer to cutting board; cool slightly. Cut into wedges. Repeat with remaining ingredients. Serve with additional pico de gallo, sour cream and guacamole.

RANCH DEVILED EGGS

Makes 12 servings

6 eggs

¼ cup cottage cheese

¼ cup ranch dressing

2 teaspoons Dijon mustard

¼ teaspoon salt

2 tablespoons minced fresh chives or dill

1 tablespoon diced well-drained pimientos or roasted red pepper

1. Bring medium saucepan of water to a boil over medium-high heat. Carefully add eggs; reduce heat to maintain a gentle boil. Cook 12 minutes. Drain and rinse under cold water. Peel eggs; cool completely.

2. Cut eggs in half lengthwise. Remove yolks; place in food processor. Place egg whites on serving plate.

3. Add cottage cheese, ranch dressing, mustard and salt to food processor; process until smooth. (Or, place ingredients in small bowl and mash with fork until well blended.) Stir in chives and pimientos. Spoon into egg whites. Cover and refrigerate at least 1 hour.

Pepperoni Pizza Rolls

Makes 12 rolls

1 loaf (16 ounces) frozen pizza dough or white bread dough, thawed according to package directions

½ cup pizza sauce, plus additional sauce for serving

⅓ cup chopped pepperoni or mini pepperoni slices (half of 2½-ounce package)

9 to 10 slices fontina, provolone or provolone-mozzarella blend cheese*

*For best results, use thinner cheese slices which are less than 1 ounce each.

1. Spray 12 standard (2½-inch) muffin pan cups with nonstick cooking spray.

2. Roll out dough into 12×10-inch rectangle on lightly floured surface. Spread ½ cup pizza sauce over dough, leaving ½-inch border on one long side. Sprinkle with pepperoni; top with cheese, cutting slices to fit as necessary. Starting with long side opposite ½-inch border, roll up dough jelly-roll style; pinch seam to seal.

3. Cut crosswise into 1-inch slices; place slices cut sides up in prepared muffin cups. Cover with plastic wrap; let rise in warm place 30 to 40 minutes or until nearly doubled in size. Preheat oven to 350°F.

4. Bake about 25 minutes or until golden brown. Loosen bottom and sides with small spatula or knife; remove to wire rack. Serve warm with additional sauce for dipping, if desired.

SOUPS & SALADS

Split Pea Soup

Makes 6 servings

3 cans (about 14 ounces each) chicken broth

1 package (16 ounces) dried split peas, rinsed and sorted

1 onion, diced

2 carrots, diced

8 slices bacon, crisp-cooked and crumbled, divided

1 teaspoon black pepper

1 bay leaf

½ teaspoon dried thyme

¼ teaspoon salt

Slow Cooker Directions

1. Combine broth, split peas, onion, carrots, half of bacon, pepper, bay leaf, thyme and salt in slow cooker.

2. Cover; cook on LOW 6 to 8 hours. Remove and discard bay leaf. Adjust seasonings, if desired. Garnish with remaining bacon.

Garden Potato Salad

Makes 4 servings

3 cups water

6 unpeeled new potatoes, quartered

8 ounces asparagus, cut into 1-inch slices

1¼ cups bell pepper strips

⅔ cup sour cream or plain yogurt

¼ cup sliced green onions

2 tablespoons chopped pitted black olives

1½ tablespoons chopped fresh basil *or* 1½ teaspoons dried basil

1 tablespoon chopped fresh thyme *or* 1 teaspoon dried thyme

1 tablespoon white vinegar

2 teaspoons sugar

Dash ground red pepper

1. Bring 3 cups water to a boil in large saucepan over high heat. Add potatoes; return to a boil. Reduce heat to medium-low; cover and cook 8 minutes.

2. Add asparagus and bell peppers; cover and cook 3 minutes or until potatoes are tender and asparagus and bell peppers are crisp-tender. Drain.

3. Meanwhile, combine sour cream, green onions, olives, basil, thyme, vinegar, sugar and ground red pepper in large bowl; mix well. Add vegetables; toss to coat. Cover and refrigerate at least 30 minutes or until chilled.

Hearty White Bean Soup

Makes 4 servings

2⅔ cups water, divided

1 can (about 15 ounces) Great Northern or navy beans, rinsed and drained

1 cup chopped carrots

1 cup chopped green or red bell pepper

1 cup chicken broth

½ cup chopped celery

2 tablespoons chopped fresh thyme *or* 2 teaspoons dried thyme

2 tablespoons chopped fresh marjoram *or* 2 teaspoons dried marjoram

½ teaspoon salt

½ teaspoon ground cumin

¼ teaspoon black pepper

3 tablespoons all-purpose flour

⅔ cup shredded Swiss or Cheddar cheese (optional)

1. Combine 2⅓ cups water, beans, carrots, bell pepper, broth, celery, thyme, marjoram, salt, cumin and black pepper in large saucepan; bring to a boil over high heat. Reduce heat to medium-low; cover and simmer 20 to 25 minutes or until vegetables are tender, stirring occasionally.

2. Whisk remaining ⅓ cup water into flour in small bowl until smooth. Add to saucepan; cook and stir over medium heat until soup boils and thickens. Cook and stir 1 minute. Sprinkle with cheese, if desired.

Chicken Waldorf Salad

Makes 4 servings

Dressing

- ⅓ cup balsamic vinegar
- 2 tablespoons Dijon mustard
- 2 teaspoons minced garlic
- ½ teaspoon salt
- ¼ teaspoon black pepper
- ⅔ cup extra virgin olive oil

Salad

- 8 cups mixed greens
- 1 large Granny Smith apple, cut into ½-inch pieces
- ⅔ cup diced celery
- ⅔ cup halved red seedless grapes
- 12 to 16 ounces sliced grilled chicken breasts
- ½ cup candied walnuts
- ½ cup crumbled blue cheese

1. For dressing, combine vinegar, mustard, garlic, salt and pepper in medium bowl; mix well. Slowly add oil, whisking until well blended.

2. For salad, combine mixed greens, apple, celery and grapes in large bowl. Add half of dressing; toss to coat. Top with chicken, walnuts and cheese; drizzle with additional dressing.

Beef Vegetable Soup

Makes 6 to 8 servings

1½ pounds cubed beef stew meat

¼ cup all-purpose flour

3 tablespoons vegetable oil, divided

1 onion, chopped

2 stalks celery, chopped

3 tablespoons tomato paste

2 teaspoons salt

1 teaspoon dried thyme

½ teaspoon garlic powder

¼ teaspoon black pepper

6 cups beef broth, divided

1 can (28 ounces) stewed tomatoes, undrained

1 tablespoon Worcestershire sauce

1 bay leaf

4 unpeeled red potatoes (about 1 pound), cut into 1-inch pieces

3 medium carrots, cut in half lengthwise then cut into ½-inch slices

6 ounces green beans, trimmed and cut into 1-inch pieces

1 cup frozen corn

1. Combine beef and flour in medium bowl; toss to coat. Heat 1 tablespoon oil in large saucepan or Dutch oven over medium-high heat. Cook beef in two batches about 5 minutes or until browned on all sides, adding additional 1 tablespoon oil after first batch. Transfer beef to medium bowl.

2. Heat remaining 1 tablespoon oil in saucepan. Add onion and celery; cook and stir about 5 minutes or until softened. Add tomato paste, 2 teaspoons salt, thyme, garlic powder and ¼ teaspoon pepper; cook and stir 1 minute. Stir in 1 cup broth, scraping up browned bits from bottom of saucepan. Stir in remaining 5 cups broth, tomatoes, Worcestershire sauce, bay leaf and beef; bring to a boil.

3. Reduce heat to low; cover and cook 1 hour and 20 minutes. Add potatoes and carrots; cook 15 minutes. Add green beans and corn; cook 15 minutes or until vegetables are tender. Remove and discard bay leaf. Season with additional salt and pepper.

Lentil Soup

Makes 6 to 8 servings

2 tablespoons olive oil, divided

2 medium onions, chopped

1½ teaspoons salt

4 cloves garlic, minced

¼ cup tomato paste

1 teaspoon dried oregano

½ teaspoon dried basil

¼ teaspoon dried thyme

¼ teaspoon black pepper

½ cup dry sherry or white wine

8 cups vegetable broth

2 cups water

2 cups dried lentils, rinsed and sorted

3 carrots, cut into ½-inch pieces

1 cup chopped fresh parsley

1 tablespoon balsamic vinegar

1. Heat 1 tablespoon oil in large saucepan or Dutch oven over medium heat. Add onions; cook 10 minutes, stirring occasionally. Add remaining 1 tablespoon oil and salt; cook 10 minutes or until onions are golden brown, stirring frequently.

2. Add garlic; cook and stir 1 minute. Add tomato paste, oregano, basil, thyme and pepper; cook and stir 1 minute. Stir in sherry; cook 30 seconds, scraping up browned bits from bottom of saucepan.

3. Stir in broth, water, lentils and carrots; cover and bring to a boil over high heat. Reduce heat to medium-low; cook, partially covered, 30 minutes or until lentils are tender.

4. Remove from heat; stir in parsley and vinegar.

Chopped Salad with Corn Bread Croutons

Makes 6 to 8 servings

½ loaf corn bread,* cut into 1-inch cubes

1 large sweet potato, peeled and cut into 1-inch pieces

5 tablespoons olive oil, divided

1½ teaspoons salt, divided

3 tablespoons red wine vinegar

2 tablespoons white wine vinegar

1 tablespoon maple syrup

1 clove garlic, minced

1 teaspoon dried mustard

⅛ teaspoon dried oregano

Pinch red pepper flakes

½ cup vegetable oil

1 head iceberg lettuce

1 cup halved grape tomatoes

2 green onions, thinly sliced

1 avocado, diced

½ cup coarsely chopped smoked almonds

½ cup dried cranberries

Purchase premade corn bread from the bakery at your grocery store, use your favorite recipe or prepare it from a mix.

1. Preheat oven to 350°F. Spread corn bread cubes in single layer in 13×9-inch baking pan. Bake 12 to 15 minutes or until corn bread is dry and toasted, stirring once. Remove to plate to cool.

2. Add sweet potato to same pan. Drizzle with 1 tablespoon olive oil and sprinkle with ½ teaspoon salt; toss to coat. Spread in single layer; bake 30 to 35 minutes or until browned and tender, stirring once or twice. Cool completely.

3. For dressing, whisk vinegars, maple syrup, garlic, mustard, oregano, red pepper flakes and remaining 1 teaspoon salt in medium bowl until blended. Whisk in remaining 4 tablespoons olive oil and vegetable oil in thin steady stream.

4. Remove outer lettuce leaves and core. Chop lettuce into ½-inch pieces; place in large bowl. Add tomatoes, green onions and half of dressing; mix well. Add sweet potato, avocado, almonds and cranberries; toss gently to coat. Taste and add additional dressing, if desired. Top with croutons.

Chicken Noodle Soup

Makes 8 servings

2 tablespoons butter

1 cup chopped onion

1 cup sliced carrots

½ cup diced celery

2 tablespoons vegetable oil

1 pound chicken breast tenderloins

1 pound chicken thigh fillets

4 cups chicken broth, divided

2 cups water

1 tablespoon minced fresh parsley, plus additional for garnish

1½ teaspoons salt

½ teaspoon black pepper

3 cups uncooked egg noodles

1. Melt butter in large saucepan or Dutch oven over medium-low heat. Add onion, carrots and celery; cook 15 minutes or until vegetables are soft, stirring occasionally.

2. Meanwhile, heat oil in large skillet over medium-high heat. Add chicken in single layer; cook about 12 minutes or until lightly browned and cooked through, turning once. Transfer chicken to cutting board.

3. Add 1 cup broth to skillet; cook 1 minute, scraping up browned bits from bottom of skillet. Add broth to vegetables. Stir in remaining 3 cups broth, water, 1 tablespoon parsley, salt and pepper.

4. Chop chicken into 1-inch pieces when cool enough to handle. Add to soup; bring to a boil over medium-high heat. Reduce heat to medium-low; cook 15 minutes. Add noodles; cook 15 minutes or until noodles are tender. Garnish with additional parsley.

Taco Salad

Makes 4 servings

Chili

- 1 pound ground beef
- 1 medium onion, chopped
- 1 stalk celery, chopped
- 2 medium tomatoes, chopped
- 1 jalapeño pepper,* finely chopped
- 1½ teaspoons chili powder
- 1 teaspoon salt
- 1 teaspoon ground cumin
- ½ teaspoon black pepper
- 1 can (15 ounces) tomato sauce
- 1 can (about 15 ounces) kidney beans, rinsed and drained
- 1 can (about 15 ounces) pinto beans, rinsed and drained
- 1 cup water

Salad

- 8 cups chopped romaine lettuce (large pieces)
- 2 cups diced fresh tomatoes
- 48 small round tortilla chips
- 1 cup salsa
- ½ cup sour cream
- 1 cup (4 ounces) shredded Cheddar cheese

Jalapeño peppers can sting and irritate the skin, so wear rubber gloves when handling peppers and do not touch your eyes.

1. Combine beef, onion and celery in large saucepan; cook over medium-high heat 6 to 8 minutes or until beef is no longer pink, stirring to break up meat. Drain fat.

2. Add tomatoes, jalapeño, chili powder, salt, cumin and black pepper; cook and stir 1 minute. Stir in tomato sauce, beans and water; bring to a boil. Reduce heat to medium-low; cook about 1 hour or until most of liquid is absorbed.

3. For each salad, combine 2 cups lettuce and ½ cup diced tomatoes in individual bowls. Top with 12 tortilla chips, ¾ cup chili, ¼ cup salsa and 2 tablespoons sour cream. Sprinkle with ¼ cup cheese. (Reserve remaining chili for another use.)

Rustic Vegetable Soup

Makes 8 servings

1 to 2 baking potatoes,
    cut into ½-inch pieces

1 bag (10 ounces) frozen
    mixed vegetables, thawed

1 bag (10 ounces) frozen
    cut green beans, thawed

1 medium green bell pepper,
    chopped

1 jar (16 ounces) picante sauce

1 can (about 10 ounces)
    condensed beef broth,
    undiluted

½ teaspoon sugar

¼ cup finely chopped fresh
    parsley

Slow Cooker Directions

1. Combine potatoes, mixed vegetables, green beans, bell pepper, picante sauce, broth and sugar in slow cooker.

2. Cover; cook on LOW 8 hours or on HIGH 4 hours. Stir in parsley just before serving.

Colorful Coleslaw

Makes 4 to 6 servings

¼ head green cabbage, shredded or thinly sliced

¼ head red cabbage, shredded or thinly sliced

1 small yellow or orange bell pepper, thinly sliced

1 small jicama, peeled and julienned

¼ cup thinly sliced green onions

2 tablespoons chopped fresh cilantro

¼ cup vegetable oil

¼ cup fresh lime juice

1 teaspoon salt

⅛ teaspoon black pepper

1. Combine cabbage, bell pepper, jicama, green onions and cilantro in large bowl; mix well.

2. Whisk oil, lime juice, salt and black pepper in small bowl until well blended. Pour over vegetables; toss to coat. Cover and refrigerate 2 to 6 hours for flavors to blend.

Note: This coleslaw also makes a great topping for tacos and sandwiches.

Chicken Enchilada Soup

Makes 8 to 10 servings

2 tablespoons vegetable oil, divided

1½ pounds boneless skinless chicken breasts, cut into ½-inch cubes

½ cup chopped onion

2 cloves garlic, minced

2 cans (about 14 ounces each) chicken broth

3 cups water, divided

1 cup masa harina

1 package (16 ounces) pasteurized process cheese product, cubed

1 can (10 ounces) mild red enchilada sauce

1 teaspoon chili powder

½ teaspoon salt

½ teaspoon ground cumin

Chopped fresh tomatoes

Crispy tortilla strips*

*If tortilla strips are not available, crumble tortilla chips into bite-size pieces.

1. Heat 1 tablespoon oil in large saucepan or Dutch oven over medium-high heat. Add chicken; cook and stir 10 minutes or until no longer pink. Transfer to large bowl with slotted spoon; drain fat from saucepan.

2. Heat remaining 1 tablespoon oil in same saucepan over medium-high heat. Add onion and garlic; cook and stir 3 minutes or until softened. Stir in broth.

3. Whisk 2 cups water into masa harina in large bowl until smooth. Whisk mixture into broth in saucepan. Stir in cheese product, remaining 1 cup water, enchilada sauce, chili powder, salt and cumin; bring to a boil over high heat. Add chicken. Reduce heat to medium-low; cook 30 minutes, stirring frequently. Top with tomatoes and tortilla strips.

Tomato, Avocado and Cucumber Salad

Makes 4 servings

2 tablespoons extra virgin olive oil

1 tablespoon balsamic vinegar

1 clove garlic, minced

½ teaspoon salt

¼ teaspoon black pepper

2 cups diced seeded plum tomatoes

1 small ripe avocado, cut into ½-inch chunks

½ cup chopped cucumber

⅓ cup crumbled feta cheese

4 large red leaf lettuce leaves

Chopped fresh basil (optional)

1. Whisk oil, vinegar, garlic, salt and pepper in medium bowl until well blended.

2. Add tomatoes and avocado; toss gently to coat. Stir in cucumber and cheese.

3. Arrange lettuce leaves on serving plates. Spoon salad onto lettuce leaves; top with basil, if desired.

BROCCOLI CHEESE SOUP

Makes 4 to 6 servings

6 tablespoons (¾ stick) butter

1 cup chopped onion

1 clove garlic, minced

¼ cup all-purpose flour

2 cups vegetable broth

2 cups milk

1½ teaspoons Dijon mustard

½ teaspoon salt

¼ teaspoon ground nutmeg

¼ teaspoon black pepper

⅛ teaspoon hot pepper sauce

1 package (16 ounces) frozen broccoli (5 cups)

2 carrots, shredded (1 cup)

6 ounces pasteurized process cheese product, cubed

1 cup (4 ounces) shredded sharp Cheddar cheese, plus additional for garnish

1. Melt butter in large saucepan or Dutch oven over medium-low heat. Add onion; cook and stir 8 minutes or until softened. Add garlic; cook and stir 1 minute. Increase heat to medium. Whisk in flour until smooth; cook and stir 3 minutes without browning.

2. Gradually whisk in broth and milk. Add mustard, salt, nutmeg, black pepper and hot pepper sauce; cook 15 minutes or until thickened, stirring occasionally.

3. Add broccoli; cook 15 minutes. Add carrots; cook 10 minutes or until vegetables are tender.

4. Transfer half of soup to food processor or blender; process until smooth. Return to saucepan. Add cheese product and 1 cup Cheddar; cook and stir over low heat until cheese is melted. Garnish with additional Cheddar.

BARBECUE CHICKEN SALAD

Makes 4 servings

DRESSING

¾ cup light or regular mayonnaise

⅓ cup buttermilk

¼ cup sour cream

1 tablespoon white wine vinegar

1 teaspoon sugar

¼ teaspoon salt

¼ teaspoon garlic powder

¼ teaspoon onion powder

¼ teaspoon dried parsley flakes

¼ teaspoon dried dill weed

¼ teaspoon black pepper

SALAD

12 to 16 ounces grilled chicken breast strips

½ cup barbecue sauce

4 cups chopped romaine lettuce

4 cups chopped iceberg lettuce

2 medium tomatoes, seeded and chopped

¾ cup canned or thawed frozen corn, drained

¾ cup diced jicama

¾ cup (3 ounces) shredded Monterey Jack cheese

¼ cup chopped fresh cilantro

2 green onions, sliced

1 cup crispy tortilla strips*

If tortilla strips are unavailable, crumble tortilla chips into bite-size pieces.

1. For dressing, whisk mayonnaise, buttermilk, sour cream, vinegar, sugar, salt, garlic powder, onion powder, parsley flakes, dill weed and pepper in medium bowl until well blended. Cover and refrigerate until ready to serve.

2. For salad, cut chicken strips into ½-inch pieces. Combine chicken and barbecue sauce in medium bowl; toss to coat.

3. Combine lettuce, tomatoes, corn, jicama, cheese and cilantro in large bowl. Add two thirds of dressing; toss to coat. Add remaining dressing, if necessary. Divide salad among four plates; top with chicken, green onions and tortilla strips.

Hearty Dinners

Spicy Buttermilk Oven-Fried Chicken

Makes 6 servings

1 cut-up whole chicken
   (about 3½ pounds)

2 cups buttermilk

1½ cups all-purpose flour

1 teaspoon salt

1 teaspoon ground red pepper

½ teaspoon garlic powder

¼ cup canola oil

1. Place chicken pieces in single layer in 13×9-inch baking dish. Pour buttermilk over chicken. Cover with plastic wrap; marinate in refrigerator at least 2 hours.

2. Preheat oven to 350°F. Combine flour, salt, red pepper and garlic powder in large shallow bowl; mix well. Heat oil in large skillet over medium-high heat.

3. Remove chicken pieces from buttermilk; coat with flour mixture. Place chicken in hot oil; cook about 10 minutes or until browned and crisp on all sides. Place chicken in single layer in clean 13×9-inch baking dish.

4. Bake, uncovered, 30 to 45 minutes or until chicken is cooked through (165°F).

STEAK FAJITAS

Makes 2 servings

¼ cup lime juice

¼ cup soy sauce

4 tablespoons vegetable oil, divided

2 tablespoons honey

2 tablespoons Worcestershire sauce

2 cloves garlic, minced

½ teaspoon ground red pepper

1 pound flank steak, skirt steak or top sirloin

1 medium yellow onion, halved and cut into ¼-inch slices

1 green bell pepper, cut into ¼-inch strips

1 red bell pepper, cut into ¼-inch strips

Flour tortillas, warmed

Lime wedges (optional)

Optional toppings: pico de gallo, guacamole, sour cream, and shredded lettuce

1. Combine lime juice, soy sauce, 2 tablespoons oil, honey, Worcestershire sauce, garlic and ground red pepper in medium bowl; mix well. Remove ¼ cup marinade to large bowl. Place steak in large resealable food storage bag. Pour remaining marinade over steak; seal bag and turn to coat. Marinate in refrigerator at least 2 hours or overnight. Add onion and bell peppers to bowl with ¼ cup marinade; toss to coat. Cover and refrigerate until ready to use.

2. Remove steak from marinade; discard marinade and wipe off excess from steak. Heat 1 tablespoon oil in large skillet (preferably cast iron) over medium-high heat. Cook steak about 4 minutes per side for medium rare or to desired doneness. Remove to cutting board; tent with foil and let rest 10 minutes.

3. Meanwhile, heat remaining 1 tablespoon oil in same skillet over medium-high heat. Add vegetable mixture; cook about 8 minutes or until vegetables are crisp-tender and beginning to brown in spots, stirring occasionally. (Cook in two batches if necessary; do not crowd vegetables in skillet.)

4. Cut steak into thin slices across the grain. Serve with vegetables, tortillas, lime wedges and desired toppings.

HEARTY SAUSAGE PASTA

Makes 4 servings

3 tablespoons olive oil

8 ounces Italian sausage, casings removed

1 small onion, finely chopped

1 red bell pepper, cut into ¼-inch strips

2 cloves garlic, minced

⅓ cup dry white wine

1 can (28 ounces) crushed tomatoes

1 can (8 ounces) tomato sauce

4 tablespoons chopped fresh basil, divided, plus additional for garnish

½ teaspoon salt

¼ teaspoon black pepper

⅛ teaspoon red pepper flakes

1 package (16 ounces) uncooked rigatoni or penne pasta

¼ cup grated Romano cheese

1 package (4 ounces) goat cheese, cut crosswise into 8 slices

1. Heat oil in large saucepan over medium heat. Break sausage into ½-inch pieces; add to saucepan. Cook about 5 minutes or until browned, stirring occasionally. Add onion and bell pepper; cook and stir 4 minutes or until vegetables are softened. Add garlic; cook and stir 1 minute.

2. Stir in wine; cook about 5 minutes or until most of liquid has evaporated. Stir in tomatoes, tomato sauce, 2 tablespoons basil, salt, black pepper and red pepper flakes; bring to a boil. Reduce heat to medium-low; cook 20 minutes or until sauce has thickened slightly.

3. Meanwhile, cook pasta in boiling salted water according to package directions for al dente. Add hot cooked pasta, Romano cheese and remaining 2 tablespoons basil to sauce; stir gently to coat. Cook just until heated through.

4. Top each serving with 1 to 2 slices goat cheese; garnish with additional basil.

Bourbon-Marinated Salmon

Makes 4 servings

¼ cup packed brown sugar

¼ cup bourbon

¼ cup soy sauce

2 tablespoons lime juice

1 tablespoon grated fresh ginger

1 tablespoon minced garlic

¼ teaspoon black pepper

4 salmon fillets (7 to 8 ounces each)

2 tablespoons minced green onion

1. Combine brown sugar, bourbon, soy sauce, lime juice, ginger, garlic and pepper in medium bowl; mix well. Reserve ¼ cup mixture for serving; set aside.

2. Place salmon in large resealable food storage bag. Pour remaining marinade over salmon; seal bag and turn to coat. Marinate in refrigerator 2 to 4 hours, turning occasionally.

3. Prepare grill or preheat broiler. Remove salmon from marinade; discard marinade.

4. Grill or broil salmon 10 minutes or until fish begins to flake when tested with fork. (To broil, place salmon on foil-lined baking sheet sprayed with nonstick cooking spray.) Brush with reserved marinade; sprinkle with green onion.

Smoky Baby Back Ribs

Makes 4 servings

1¼ cups water

1 cup white vinegar

⅔ cup packed dark brown sugar

½ cup tomato paste

1 tablespoon yellow mustard

1½ teaspoons salt

1 teaspoon liquid smoke

1 teaspoon onion powder

½ teaspoon garlic powder

½ teaspoon paprika

2 racks pork baby back ribs
(3½ to 4 pounds total)

1. Combine water, vinegar, brown sugar, tomato paste, mustard, salt, liquid smoke, onion powder, garlic powder and paprika in medium saucepan; bring to a boil over medium heat. Reduce heat to medium-low; cook 40 minutes or until sauce thickens, stirring occasionally.

2. Preheat oven to 300°F. Place each rack of ribs on large sheet of heavy-duty foil. Brush some of sauce over ribs, covering completely. Fold down edges of foil tightly to seal and create packet; arrange packets on baking sheet, seam sides up.

3. Bake 2 hours. Prepare grill or preheat broiler. Carefully drain off excess liquid from rib packets.

4. Brush ribs with sauce; grill or broil about 5 minutes per side or until beginning to char, brushing with sauce once or twice during grilling. Serve with remaining sauce.

Vegetable Enchiladas

Makes 6 servings

1 tablespoon vegetable oil

2 large poblano peppers or green bell peppers, cut into ¼-inch slices

1 large zucchini, cut into thin strips (about 3 × ¼ inches)

1 large red onion, cut in half then cut into ¼-inch slices

1 cup sliced mushrooms

1 teaspoon ground cumin

1 pound fresh tomatillos (about 8 large), peeled

½ to 1 jalapeño pepper,* minced

1 clove garlic

½ teaspoon salt

1 cup loosely packed fresh cilantro, plus additional for garnish

12 corn tortillas, warmed

2 cups (8 ounces) shredded Mexican cheese blend, divided

*Jalapeño peppers can sting and irritate the skin, so wear rubber gloves when handling peppers and do not touch your eyes.

1. Preheat oven to 400°F.

2. Heat oil in large nonstick skillet over medium heat. Add poblano peppers, zucchini, onion, mushrooms and cumin; cook and stir 8 to 10 minutes or until vegetables are crisp-tender.

3. Meanwhile, place tomatillos in large microwavable bowl. Cover with vented plastic wrap. Microwave on HIGH 6 to 7 minutes or until very tender.

4. Combine tomatillos with juice, jalapeño, garlic and salt in food processor or blender; process until smooth. Add 1 cup cilantro; pulse until combined and cilantro is coarsely chopped.

5. Divide vegetables evenly among tortillas. Spoon heaping tablespoon of cheese in center of each tortilla; roll up to enclose filling. Place in 13 × 9-inch baking dish. Pour sauce over enchiladas; sprinkle with remaining 1 cup cheese.

6. Cover and bake 18 to 20 minutes or until cheese is melted and enchiladas are heated through. Garnish with additional cilantro. Serve immediately.

CHICKEN AND HERB STEW

Makes 4 servings

½ cup all-purpose flour

½ teaspoon salt

¼ teaspoon black pepper

¼ teaspoon paprika

4 chicken drumsticks

4 chicken thighs

2 tablespoons olive oil

12 ounces unpeeled new potatoes, quartered

2 carrots, quartered lengthwise, then cut crosswise into 3-inch pieces

1 green bell pepper, cut into thin strips

¾ cup chopped onion

2 cloves garlic, minced

1¾ cups water

¼ cup dry white wine

2 cubes chicken bouillon

1 tablespoon chopped fresh oregano

1 teaspoon chopped fresh rosemary leaves

2 tablespoons chopped fresh Italian parsley (optional)

1. Combine flour, salt, black pepper and paprika in shallow dish; stir until well blended. Coat chicken with flour mixture; shake off excess.

2. Heat oil in large skillet over medium-high heat. Add chicken; cook about 6 minutes per side or until browned. Remove to plate.

3. Add potatoes, carrots, bell pepper, onion and garlic to skillet; cook and stir 6 minutes or until vegetables are lightly browned. Add water, wine and bouillon; cook 1 minute, scraping up browned bits from bottom of skillet. Stir in oregano and rosemary.

4. Place chicken on top of vegetable mixture, turning several times to coat. Cover and cook 45 to 50 minutes or until chicken is cooked through (165°F), turning occasionally. Garnish with parsley.

Corn Chip Chili

Makes 6 servings

1 tablespoon olive oil

1 medium onion, chopped

1 medium red bell pepper, chopped

1 jalapeno pepper,* seeded and finely chopped

4 cloves garlic, minced

2 pounds ground beef

1 can (4 ounces) diced green chiles, drained

2 cans (about 14 ounces each) fire-roasted diced tomatoes

2 tablespoons chili powder

1½ teaspoons ground cumin

1½ teaspoons dried oregano

¾ teaspoon salt

3 cups corn chips

1 cup (4 ounces) shredded sharp Cheddar cheese

6 tablespoons chopped green onions

Jalapeño peppers can sting and irritate the skin, so wear rubber gloves when handling peppers and do not touch your eyes.

Slow Cooker Directions

1. Heat oil in large skillet over medium-high heat. Add onion, bell pepper, jalapeño and garlic; cook and stir 3 minutes or until softened. Add beef; cook and stir 10 to 12 minutes or until beef is no longer pink and liquid has evaporated. Stir in green chiles; cook 1 minute. Transfer to slow cooker; stir in tomatoes, chili powder, cumin, oregano and salt.

2. Cover; cook on LOW 6 to 7 hours or on HIGH 3 to 3½ hours.

3. Place corn chips in serving bowls; top with chili. Sprinkle with cheese and green onions.

Meatballs and Ricotta

Makes 5 to 6 servings (20 meatballs)

Meatballs

- 2 tablespoons olive oil
- ½ cup plain dry bread crumbs
- ½ cup milk
- 1 cup finely chopped yellow onion
- 2 green onions, finely chopped
- ½ cup grated Romano cheese, plus additional for serving
- 2 eggs, beaten
- ¼ cup finely chopped fresh parsley
- ¼ cup finely chopped fresh basil
- 2 cloves garlic, minced
- 2 teaspoons salt
- ¼ teaspoon black pepper
- 1 pound ground beef
- 1 pound ground pork

Sauce

- 2 tablespoons olive oil
- 2 tablespoons butter
- 1 cup finely chopped yellow onion
- 1 clove garlic, minced
- 1 can (28 ounces) whole Italian plum tomatoes, coarsely chopped, juice reserved
- 1 can (28 ounces) crushed tomatoes
- 1 teaspoon salt
- ¼ teaspoon black pepper
- ¼ cup finely chopped fresh basil
- 1 to 1½ cups ricotta cheese

1. Preheat oven to 375°F. Brush 2 tablespoons oil over large rimmed baking sheet.

2. Combine bread crumbs and milk in large bowl; mix well. Add 1 cup yellow onion, green onions, ½ cup Romano, eggs, parsley, ¼ cup basil, 2 cloves garlic, 2 teaspoons salt and ¼ teaspoon black pepper; mix well. Add beef and pork; mix gently but thoroughly until blended. Shape mixture by ¼ cupfuls into balls. Place meatballs on prepared baking sheet; turn to coat with oil.

3. Bake about 20 minutes or until meatballs are cooked through (165°F). Meanwhile, prepare sauce.

4. Heat 2 tablespoons oil and butter in large saucepan over medium heat until butter is melted. Add 1 cup yellow onion; cook 8 minutes or until tender and lightly browned, stirring frequently. Add 1 clove garlic; cook and stir 1 minute or until fragrant. Add plum tomatoes with juice, crushed tomatoes, 1 teaspoon salt and ¼ teaspoon black pepper; bring to a simmer. Reduce heat to medium-low; cook 20 minutes, stirring occasionally.

5. Stir ¼ cup basil into sauce. Add meatballs; cook 10 minutes, stirring occasionally. Transfer meatballs and sauce to serving dish; dollop tablespoonfuls of ricotta between meatballs. Garnish with additional Romano.

Cheesy Chicken with Mushrooms and Bacon

Makes 4 servings

½ cup honey

½ cup Dijon mustard

2 tablespoons vegetable oil, divided

1 teaspoon lemon juice

4 boneless skinless chicken breasts (about 6 ounces each)

Salt and black pepper

1 tablespoon butter

2 cups sliced mushrooms

4 slices bacon, cooked

½ cup (2 ounces) shredded Cheddar cheese

½ cup (2 ounces) shredded Monterey Jack cheese

Chopped fresh parsley

1. Whisk honey, mustard, 1 tablespoon oil and lemon juice in medium bowl until well blended. Reserve half of marinade mixture to use as sauce; cover and refrigerate until ready to serve.

2. Place chicken in large resealable food storage bag. Pour remaining half of marinade over chicken; seal bag and turn to coat. Refrigerate at least 2 hours.

3. Preheat oven to 375°F. Remove chicken from marinade; discard marinade. Heat remaining 1 tablespoon oil in large ovenproof skillet over medium-high heat. Add chicken; cook 3 to 4 minutes per side or until golden brown. (Chicken will not be cooked through.) Remove to plate; sprinkle with salt and pepper.

4. Heat butter in same skillet over medium-high heat. Add mushrooms; cook 8 minutes or until mushrooms begin to brown, stirring occasionally and scraping up browned bits from bottom of skillet. Season with salt and pepper. Return chicken to skillet; spoon mushrooms over chicken. Top with bacon; sprinkle with Cheddar and Monterey Jack.

5. Bake 8 to 10 minutes or until chicken is no longer pink in center and cheeses are melted. Sprinkle with parsley; serve with reserved honey-mustard mixture.

Cowboy Barbecue Burgers

Makes 4 servings

1½ pounds ground beef

1 cup smokehouse-style barbecue sauce

¼ cup brown ale

½ teaspoon salt

¼ teaspoon black pepper

1 red onion, cut into ½-inch-thick slices

4 hamburger buns

8 slices thick-cut bacon, crisp-cooked

Lettuce leaves

Tomato slices

1. Prepare grill for direct cooking. Shape beef into four patties about ¾ inch thick.

2. Combine barbecue sauce, ale, salt and pepper in small saucepan. Bring to a boil over medium heat; boil 1 minute. Set aside.

3. Grill burgers, covered, over medium-high heat 8 to 10 minutes for medium (160°F) or to desired doneness, turning occasionally. Grill onion 4 minutes or until softened and slightly charred, turning occasionally.

4. Serve burgers on buns with onion, bacon, barbecue sauce mixture, lettuce and tomatoes.

Tuna Tomato Casserole

Makes 6 servings

2 cans (6 ounces each) tuna, drained and flaked

1 cup mayonnaise

1 onion, finely chopped

¼ teaspoon salt

¼ teaspoon black pepper

1 package (12 ounces) wide egg noodles, uncooked

8 to 10 plum tomatoes, cut into ¼-inch slices

1 cup (4 ounces) shredded Cheddar or mozzarella cheese

1. Preheat oven to 375°F.

2. Combine tuna, mayonnaise, onion, salt and pepper in medium bowl; mix well.

3. Cook noodles according to package directions; drain and return to saucepan. Gently stir in tuna mixture until well blended. Layer half of noodle mixture, half of tomatoes and half of cheese in 13×9-inch baking dish; press down slightly. Repeat layers.

4. Bake 20 minutes or until cheese is melted and casserole is heated through.

Pork Chops and Stuffing Skillet

Makes 4 servings

4 thin bone-in pork chops (1 pound)

¼ teaspoon dried thyme

¼ teaspoon paprika

⅛ teaspoon salt

1 tablespoon vegetable oil

4 ounces bulk pork sausage

2 cups corn bread stuffing mix

1¼ cups water

1 cup diced green bell peppers

⅛ to ¼ teaspoon poultry seasoning (optional)

1. Preheat oven to 350°F. Sprinkle one side of pork chops with thyme, paprika and salt.

2. Heat oil in large ovenproof skillet over medium-high heat. Add pork, seasoned side down; cook 2 minutes. Remove to plate.

3. Add sausage to skillet; cook 6 to 8 minutes or until no longer pink, stirring to break up meat. Remove from heat; stir in stuffing mix, water, bell peppers and poultry seasoning, if desired, until just blended. Arrange pork, seasoned side up, over stuffing mixture.

4. Cover and bake 15 minutes or until pork is barely pink in center. Let stand 5 minutes before serving.

Eggplant Parmesan

Makes 4 servings

- 2 tablespoons olive oil
- 2 cloves garlic, minced
- 1 can (28 ounces) Italian whole tomatoes, undrained
- ½ cup water
- 1¼ teaspoons salt, divided
- ¼ teaspoon dried oregano
- Pinch red pepper flakes
- 1 medium eggplant (about 1 pound)
- ⅓ cup all-purpose flour

- Black pepper
- ⅔ cup milk
- 1 egg
- 1 cup Italian-seasoned dry bread crumbs
- 4 to 5 tablespoons vegetable oil, divided
- 1 cup (4 ounces) shredded mozzarella cheese
- Chopped fresh parsley

1. Heat olive oil in medium saucepan over medium heat. Add garlic; cook and stir 2 minutes or until softened (do not brown). Crush tomatoes with hands (in bowl or in can); add to saucepan with juices from can. Stir in water, 1 teaspoon salt, oregano and red pepper flakes; bring to a simmer. Reduce heat to medium-low; cook 45 minutes, stirring occasionally.

2. Meanwhile, prepare eggplant. Cut eggplant crosswise into ¼-inch slices. Combine flour, remaining ¼ teaspoon salt and black pepper in shallow dish. Beat milk and egg in another shallow dish. Place bread crumbs in third shallow dish.

3. Coat both sides of eggplant slices with flour mixture, shaking off excess. Dip in egg mixture, letting excess drip back into dish. Roll in bread crumbs to coat. Place eggplant slices in single layer on baking sheet. Preheat broiler.

4. Heat 3 tablespoons vegetable oil in large skillet over medium-high heat. Working in batches, add eggplant slices to skillet in single layer;

cook 3 to 4 minutes per side or until golden brown, adding additional vegetable oil as needed. Remove to paper towel-lined plate; cover loosely with foil to keep warm.

5. Spray 13×9-inch baking dish with nonstick cooking spray. Arrange eggplant slices overlapping in baking dish; top with half of warm marinara sauce. (Reserve remaining marinara sauce for pasta or another use.) Sprinkle with cheese.

6. Broil 2 to 3 minutes or just until cheese is melted and beginning to brown. Garnish with parsley.

CHICKEN SCALOPPINE WITH MUSHROOMS AND ARTICHOKES

Makes 4 servings

½ cup all-purpose flour

½ teaspoon salt

¼ teaspoon black pepper

4 boneless skinless chicken breasts (about 6 ounces each)

5 tablespoons butter, divided

2 tablespoons olive oil, divided

1 package (3 to 4 ounces) diced pancetta *or* ⅓ cup diced prosciutto

1 pound sliced mushrooms

1 can (14 ounces) artichoke hearts, drained and sliced

3 tablespoons capers, rinsed and drained

⅓ cup lemon juice

3 tablespoons dry white wine

¾ cup whipping cream

2 teaspoons cornstarch

¾ cup chicken broth

Additional black pepper

1 package (16 ounces) angel hair pasta, cooked and drained

Chopped fresh parsley (optional)

1. Preheat oven to 250°F. Line baking sheet with foil. Combine flour, ½ teaspoon salt and ¼ teaspoon pepper in shallow dish. Pound chicken to ⅛-inch thickness between sheets of waxed paper with meat mallet or rolling pin. Cut each chicken breast in half crosswise. Coat both sides of chicken with flour mixture, shaking off excess.

2. Heat 1 tablespoon butter and 1 tablespoon oil in large skillet over medium-high heat. Add chicken in single layer; cook about 3 minutes per side or until golden brown. (Cook chicken in batches if necessary.) Remove to prepared baking sheet; place in oven to keep warm.

3. Add pancetta to skillet; cook and stir over medium heat 3 minutes or until lightly browned, scraping up browned bits from bottom of skillet. Add

mushrooms; cook about 8 minutes or until mushrooms begin to brown, stirring occasionally. (Add additional 1 tablespoon oil if necessary to cook mushrooms.) Stir in artichokes and capers; cook 4 minutes. Reduce heat to low while preparing sauce.

4. Combine lemon juice and wine in small saucepan; bring to a boil over medium-high heat. Boil until reduced by one third. Stir in cream; cook over medium heat 4 minutes or until slightly thickened. Stir cornstarch into broth in small bowl until blended. Add to saucepan; cook and stir 3 minutes or until sauce thickens. Add remaining 4 tablespoons butter, 1 tablespoon at a time, stirring until sauce is smooth and well blended. Add sauce to mushroom mixture; cook and stir until heated through. Season with additional pepper.

5. Divide pasta among four plates; top with chicken and mushroom mixture. Garnish with parsley.

CHEESEBURGER POTATO CASSEROLE

Makes 6 servings

- 1 pound ground beef
- ½ cup chopped onion
- 1 can (about 10¾ ounces) Cheddar cheese soup
- ¼ cup sweet pickle relish
- 2 tablespoons brown mustard
- 2 tablespoons ketchup, plus additional for topping
- 1 tablespoon Worcestershire sauce
- 1 package (30 ounces) shredded potatoes
- 2 cups (8 ounces) shredded Cheddar cheese
- 1 teaspoon salt
- ½ teaspoon black pepper
- Green onions (optional)

SLOW COOKER DIRECTIONS

1. Brown beef and onion in large skillet over medium-high heat 6 to 8 minutes, stirring to break up meat. Drain fat. Stir in cheese soup, relish, mustard, 2 tablespoons ketchup and Worcestershire sauce until well blended.

2. Arrange half of potatoes in bottom of slow cooker; top with half of beef mixture. Sprinkle with 1½ cups cheese, ½ teaspoon salt and ¼ teaspoon pepper. Repeat potato and beef layers; sprinkle with remaining ½ cup cheese, salt and pepper.

3. Cover; cook on LOW 4 hours or on HIGH 2 hours. Top with additional ketchup and green onions, if desired.

VEGETABLES & SIDES

HEARTY HASH BROWN CASSEROLE

Makes about 16 servings

2 cups sour cream

2 cups (8 ounces) shredded Colby cheese, divided

1 can (10¾ ounces) cream of chicken soup

½ cup (1 stick) butter, melted

1 small onion, finely chopped

¾ teaspoon salt

½ teaspoon black pepper

1 package (30 ounces) frozen shredded hash brown potatoes, thawed

1. Preheat oven to 375°F. Spray 13×9-inch baking dish with nonstick cooking spray.

2. Combine sour cream, 1½ cups cheese, soup, butter, onion, salt and pepper in large bowl; mix well. Add potatoes; stir until well blended. Spread mixture in prepared baking dish. (Do not pack down.) Sprinkle with remaining ½ cup cheese.

3. Bake about 45 minutes or until cheese is melted and top of casserole is beginning to brown.

Roasted Root Vegetables

Makes 6 servings

2 sweet potatoes (about 1 pound), scrubbed, peeled and cut into ½-inch wedges

3 turnips (about 8 ounces), peeled and cut into ½-inch wedges

1 medium red onion, cut into ½-inch wedges

1½ cups baby carrots

3 tablespoons olive oil

4 cloves garlic, minced

½ teaspoon salt

¼ teaspoon black pepper

1. Preheat oven to 425°F. Combine sweet potatoes, turnips, onion and carrots in large bowl. Add oil, garlic, salt and pepper; toss to coat. Spread vegetables in single layer on two baking sheets.

2. Roast 40 to 45 minutes or until vegetables are tender and browned; stirring occasionally.

Green Beans with Garlic-Cilantro Butter

Makes 4 to 6 servings

1½ pounds green beans, trimmed

3 tablespoons butter

1 red bell pepper, cut into thin strips

½ sweet onion, halved and thinly sliced

2 teaspoons minced garlic

1 teaspoon salt

2 tablespoons chopped fresh cilantro

Black pepper

1. Bring large saucepan of salted water to a boil over medium-high heat. Add beans; cook 6 minutes or until tender. Drain beans.

2. Meanwhile, melt butter in large skillet over medium-high heat. Add bell pepper and onion; cook and stir 3 minutes or until vegetables are tender but not browned. Add garlic; cook and stir 30 seconds. Add beans and salt; cook and stir 2 minutes or until beans are heated through and coated with butter. Stir in cilantro; season with black pepper. Serve immediately.

Quick Mushroom Pilaf

Makes 4 servings

2 tablespoons butter, divided

1 package (3 ounces) Asian-flavored ramen noodles, crumbled

½ cup chopped pecans

1 package (8 ounces) sliced mushrooms

2 cups hot cooked rice

2 tablespoons chopped fresh parsley

1. Melt 1 tablespoon butter in large skillet over medium-high heat. Add ramen noodles and pecans; cook and stir 3 minutes or until toasted. Remove to plate.

2. Melt remaining 1 tablespoon butter in skillet. Add mushrooms; cook 8 minutes or until browned, stirring occasionally.

3. Add rice, ramen seasoning packet, noodle mixture and parsley; cook and stir 2 minutes or until heated through.

Tip: Add 2 cups chopped cooked chicken to the pilaf to make a main dish.

GARLIC KNOTS

Makes 20 knots

¾ cup warm water (105° to 115°F)

1 package (¼ ounce) active dry yeast

1 teaspoon sugar

2¼ cups all-purpose flour, plus additional for work surface

2 tablespoons olive oil, divided

1½ teaspoons salt, divided

4 tablespoons (½ stick) butter, divided

1 tablespoon minced garlic

¼ teaspoon garlic powder

½ cup grated Parmesan cheese

2 tablespoons chopped fresh parsley

½ teaspoon dried oregano

1. Combine water, yeast and sugar in large bowl of electric stand mixer; stir to dissolve yeast. Let stand 5 minutes or until bubbly. Stir in 2¼ cups flour, 1 tablespoon oil and 1 teaspoon salt; knead with dough hook at low speed 5 minutes or until dough is smooth and elastic. Shape dough into a ball. Place in large lightly greased bowl; turn to grease top. Cover and let rise 1 hour or until doubled in size.

2. Melt 2 tablespoons butter in small saucepan over low heat. Add remaining 1 tablespoon oil, ½ teaspoon salt, minced garlic and garlic powder; cook over very low heat 5 minutes. Pour into small bowl; set aside.

3. Preheat oven to 400°F. Line baking sheet with parchment paper.

4. Turn out dough onto lightly floured surface. Punch down dough; let stand 10 minutes. Roll out dough into 10×8-inch rectangle. Cut into 20 (2-inch) squares. Roll each piece into 8-inch rope; tie in a knot. Place knots on prepared baking sheet; brush with garlic mixture.

5. Bake 10 minutes or until knots are lightly browned. Meanwhile, melt remaining 2 tablespoons butter. Combine cheese, parsley and oregano in small bowl; mix well. Brush melted butter over baked knots; immediately sprinkle with cheese mixture. Cool slightly; serve warm.

CHEESY SPINACH CASSEROLE

Makes 6 servings

1 pound baby spinach

4 slices bacon, chopped

1 small onion, chopped

1 cup sliced mushrooms

¼ cup chopped red bell pepper

3 cloves garlic, minced

1½ teaspoons minced canned chipotle peppers in adobo sauce

1 teaspoon seasoned salt

8 ounces pasteurized process cheese product, cut into pieces

½ (8-ounce) package cream cheese, cut into pieces

1 cup thawed frozen corn

½ cup (2 ounces) shredded Monterey Jack and Cheddar cheese blend

1. Preheat oven to 350°F. Spray 1-quart baking dish with nonstick cooking spray.

2. Heat large saucepan of water to a boil over high heat. Add spinach; cook 1 minute. Drain and transfer to bowl of ice water to stop cooking. Drain and squeeze spinach dry; set aside. Wipe out saucepan with paper towel.

3. Cook bacon in same saucepan over medium-high heat until almost crisp, stirring frequently. Drain off all but 1 tablespoon drippings. Add onion to saucepan; cook and stir 3 minutes or until softened. Add mushrooms and bell pepper; cook and stir 5 minutes or until vegetables are tender. Add garlic, chipotle and seasoned salt; cook and stir 1 minute.

4. Add process cheese and cream cheese to saucepan; cook over medium heat until melted, stirring frequently. Add spinach and corn; cook and stir 3 minutes. Transfer to prepared baking dish; sprinkle with shredded cheese.

5. Bake 20 to 25 minutes or until cheese is melted and casserole is bubbly. If desired, broil 1 to 2 minutes to brown top of casserole.

Loaded Baked Potatoes

Makes 4 servings

4 large baking potatoes

1 cup (4 ounces) shredded Cheddar cheese

1 cup (4 ounces) shredded Monterey Jack cheese

8 slices bacon, crisp-cooked

½ cup sour cream

¼ cup (½ stick) butter, melted

2 tablespoons milk

1 teaspoon salt

¼ teaspoon black pepper

1 tablespoon vegetable oil

2 teaspoons coarse sea salt

1 green onion, thinly sliced

1. Preheat oven to 400°F. Poke potatoes all over with fork; place in small baking pan. Bake about 1 hour or until potatoes are fork-tender. Let stand until cool enough to handle. *Reduce oven temperature to 350°F.*

2. Combine Cheddar and Monterey Jack in small bowl; reserve ¼ cup for garnish. Chop bacon; reserve ¼ cup for garnish.

3. Cut off thin slice from one long side of each potato. Scoop out centers of potatoes, leaving ¼-inch shell. Place flesh from 3 potatoes in medium bowl. (Reserve flesh from fourth potato for another use.) Add sour cream, butter, remaining 1¾ cups shredded cheese, bacon, milk, 1 teaspoon salt and pepper to bowl with potatoes; mash until well blended.

4. Turn potato shells over; brush bottoms and sides with oil. Sprinkle evenly with sea salt. Turn right side up and return to baking pan. Fill shells with mashed potato mixture, mounding over tops of shells. Sprinkle with reserved cheese and bacon.

5. Bake about 20 minutes or until filling is hot and cheese is melted. Garnish with green onion.

Classic Macaroni and Cheese

Makes 8 servings

2 cups uncooked elbow macaroni

¼ cup (½ stick) butter

¼ cup all-purpose flour

2½ cups whole milk

1 teaspoon salt

⅛ teaspoon black pepper

4 cups (16 ounces) shredded Colby-Jack cheese

1. Cook pasta according to package directions until al dente; drain.

2. Melt butter in large saucepan over medium heat. Add flour; whisk until well blended and bubbly. Gradually add milk, salt and pepper; whisk until blended. Cook and stir until milk begins to bubble. Add cheese, 1 cup at a time; cook and stir until cheese is melted and sauce is smooth.

3. Add cooked pasta to saucepan; stir gently until blended. Cook until heated through.

Jalapeño Beans

Makes 4 to 6 servings

1 tablespoon vegetable oil

1 small onion, finely chopped

1 teaspoon ground cumin

1 teaspoon garlic powder

½ teaspoon smoked paprika

¼ teaspoon ground red pepper

3 tablespoons chopped pickled jalapeño peppers

2 cans (about 15 ounces each) chili beans (made with pinto beans)

⅓ cup dark lager beer

1 tablespoon white vinegar

1 teaspoon sugar

½ teaspoon hot pepper sauce

Salt and black pepper

1. Heat oil in medium saucepan over medium-high heat. Add onion; cook and stir 2 minutes or until translucent. Add cumin, garlic powder, paprika and red pepper; cook and stir 1 minute. Add pickled jalapeños; cook and stir 30 seconds.

2. Stir in beans, beer, vinegar, sugar and hot pepper sauce; bring to a boil. Reduce heat to medium-low; cook 15 minutes, stirring occasionally. Season with salt and black pepper. Beans will thicken upon standing.

Easy Dirty Rice

Makes 4 servings

½ pound bulk Italian sausage

2 cups water

1 cup uncooked long grain rice

1 large onion, finely chopped

1 large green bell pepper, finely chopped

½ cup finely chopped celery

1½ teaspoons salt

½ teaspoon ground red pepper

½ cup chopped fresh parsley

Slow Cooker Directions

1. Brown sausage in skillet over medium-high heat 6 to 8 minutes, stirring to break up meat. Drain fat.

2. Transfer sausage to slow cooker; stir in water, rice, onion, bell pepper, celery, salt and ground red pepper.

3. Cover; cook on LOW 2 hours. Stir in parsley.

Ham-Seasoned Peas

Makes 4 servings

1 tablespoon olive oil	¼ cup chicken broth
½ cup chopped cooked ham	¼ teaspoon salt
¼ cup chopped onion	⅛ teaspoon dried oregano
2 cups frozen peas	⅛ teaspoon black pepper

1. Heat oil in medium saucepan over medium heat. Add ham and onion; cook and stir 2 minutes or until onion is tender.

2. Stir in peas, broth, salt, oregano and pepper; bring to a boil. Reduce heat to low; cover and cook 4 minutes or until peas are tender.

Smashed Potatoes

Makes 4 servings

4 medium russet potatoes
(about 1½ pounds), peeled
and cut into ¼-inch cubes

⅓ cup milk

2 tablespoons sour cream

1 tablespoon minced onion

½ teaspoon salt

¼ teaspoon black pepper

⅛ teaspoon garlic powder

Chopped fresh chives
or French fried onions
(optional)

1. Bring large saucepan of lightly salted water to a boil. Add potatoes; cook 15 to 20 minutes or until fork-tender. Drain and return to saucepan.

2. Slightly mash potatoes. Stir in milk, sour cream, minced onion, salt, pepper and garlic powder. Mash until desired texture is reached, leaving potatoes chunky. Cook 5 minutes over low heat until heated through, stirring occasionally. Top with chives, if desired.

Old-Fashioned Herb Stuffing

Makes 4 servings

6 slices (8 ounces) whole wheat, rye or white bread (or a combination), cut into ½-inch cubes

1 tablespoon butter

1 cup chopped onion

½ cup thinly sliced celery

½ cup thinly sliced carrot

1 cup chicken broth

1 tablespoon chopped fresh thyme *or* 1 teaspoon dried thyme

1 tablespoon chopped fresh sage *or* 1 teaspoon dried sage

½ teaspoon paprika

¼ teaspoon black pepper

1. Preheat oven to 350°F. Spray 1½-quart baking dish with nonstick cooking spray.

2. Place bread cubes on baking sheet; bake 10 minutes or until dry.

3. Melt butter in large saucepan over medium heat. Add onion, celery and carrot; cook and stir 10 minutes or until vegetables are tender. Add broth, thyme, sage, paprika and pepper; bring to a simmer. Stir in bread cubes. Spoon into prepared baking dish.

4. Cover and bake 25 to 30 minutes or until heated through.

Hush Puppies

Makes about 24 hush puppies

1½ cups yellow cornmeal	1 small onion, minced
½ cup all-purpose flour	1 egg, lightly beaten
2 teaspoons baking powder	Vegetable oil
¾ teaspoon salt	Ketchup (optional)
1 cup milk	

1. Combine cornmeal, flour, baking powder and salt in medium bowl; mix well. Add milk, onion and egg; stir until well blended. Let batter stand 5 to 10 minutes.

2. Heat 1 inch oil in large heavy skillet over medium heat to 375°F; adjust heat to maintain temperature. Drop batter by tablespoonfuls into hot oil. Cook, in batches, 2 minutes or until golden brown. Drain on paper towel-lined plate. Serve warm with ketchup, if desired.

Cheddar Broccoli Casserole with Crunchy Topping

Makes 8 servings

1 can (10¾ ounces) condensed cream of mushroom soup

1 cup (4 ounces) shredded Cheddar cheese

2 eggs

¼ cup sour cream or plain Greek yogurt

1 teaspoon salt

1 can (5 ounces) sliced water chestnuts, drained

½ cup chopped onion

2 packages (9 ounces each) frozen chopped broccoli, thawed

8 round butter crackers, crushed

1 tablespoon melted butter

1. Preheat oven to 350°F. Spray 2-quart casserole with nonstick cooking spray.

2. Combine soup, cheese, eggs, sour cream and salt in large bowl; mix well. Stir in water chestnuts and onion. Fold in broccoli until blended. Pour into prepared casserole.

3. Bake 30 minutes.

4. Combine crackers and butter in small bowl; mix well. Sprinkle evenly over casserole. Bake 5 minutes or until lightly browned. Let stand 10 minutes before serving.

Oven-Roasted Herbed Potatoes

Makes 6 servings

3 pounds unpeeled red potatoes, cut into 1½-inch pieces

1 sweet onion, such as Vidalia or Walla Walla, coarsely chopped

3 tablespoons olive oil

2 tablespoons melted butter or bacon drippings

3 cloves garlic, minced

¾ teaspoon salt

¾ teaspoon black pepper

⅓ cup packed chopped mixed fresh herbs, such as basil, chives, parsley, oregano, rosemary leaves, sage, tarragon and thyme

1. Preheat oven to 450°F. Line baking sheet or shallow roasting pan with foil.

2. Combine potatoes and onion on prepared baking sheet. Combine oil, butter, garlic, salt and pepper in small bowl; mix well. Drizzle over vegetables; toss to coat. Spread in single layer.

3. Roast 30 minutes. Stir vegetables; roast 10 minutes. Add herbs; toss to coat. Roast 10 minutes or until vegetables are tender and browned.

DESSERTS & SWEETS

TRIPLE BERRY COOKIE COBBLER

Makes 12 servings

4 cups sliced fresh strawberries

4 cups fresh blueberries

3 cups fresh blackberries

¾ cup sugar

3½ tablespoons cornstarch

½ teaspoon ground cinnamon

12 ready-to-bake refrigerated sugar cookies (half of 16-ounce package)*

Reserve remaining half of package for another use.

1. Position rack in upper third of oven. Preheat oven to 350°F.

2. Combine berries, sugar, cornstarch and cinnamon in large bowl; toss gently to coat. Spoon into 13×9-inch baking dish.

3. Bake 10 minutes. Remove from oven; crumble cookie dough over fruit mixture. Bake 45 to 50 minutes or until filling is bubbly and cookie dough is crisp and golden brown.

Autumn Apple Bars

Makes about 3 dozen bars

1 package (15 ounces) refrigerated pie crusts (2 crusts)

1 cup graham cracker crumbs

8 tart cooking apples, peeled and sliced ¼ inch thick (8 cups)

1 cup plus 2 tablespoons granulated sugar, divided

2½ teaspoons ground cinnamon, divided

¼ teaspoon ground nutmeg

1 egg white

1 cup powdered sugar

1 to 2 tablespoons milk

½ teaspoon vanilla

1. Preheat oven to 350°F. Roll out one pie crust to 15×10-inch rectangle on lightly floured surface. Place on bottom of ungreased 15×10-inch jelly-roll pan.

2. Sprinkle graham cracker crumbs over dough; layer apple slices over crumbs. Combine 1 cup granulated sugar, 1½ teaspoons cinnamon and nutmeg in small bowl; sprinkle over apples.

3. Roll out remaining pie crust to 15×10-inch rectangle; place over apple layer. Beat egg white in small bowl until foamy; brush over top crust. Combine remaining 2 tablespoons granulated sugar and remaining 1 teaspoon cinnamon in separate small bowl; sprinkle over crust.

4. Bake 45 minutes or until lightly browned. Cool in pan on wire rack.

5. Combine powdered sugar, 1 tablespoon milk and vanilla in small bowl. Add additional milk, if necessary, to reach desired consistency. Drizzle over top.

Banana Oatmeal Cookies

Makes about 2 dozen cookies

1 cup raisins

⅓ cup boiling water

2 cups quick oats

2 cups all-purpose flour

1 tablespoon ground cinnamon

1 tablespoon apple pie spice

1 teaspoon baking soda

1 teaspoon salt

1½ cups sugar

¾ cup shortening

2 eggs

3 bananas, mashed

¼ cup milk

½ cup chopped pecans

1. Preheat oven to 375°F. Place raisins in small bowl. Pour boiling water over raisins; set aside.

2. Combine oats, flour, cinnamon, apple pie spice, baking soda and salt in medium bowl; mix well. Beat sugar and shortening in large bowl with electric mixer at medium speed until creamy. Add eggs, one at a time, beating well after each addition. Add bananas and milk, beating until fluffy. Gradually add oat mixture; beat on low speed until stiff dough forms.

3. Drain raisins; stir raisins and pecans into dough. Drop dough by heaping tablespoonfuls 2 inches apart onto ungreased cookie sheets.

4. Bake 12 to 15 minutes or until edges are set and lightly browned. Cool on cookie sheets 1 minute; remove to wire racks to cool completely.

BROWN BUTTER BLUEBERRY PEACH COBBLER

Makes 8 servings

3 tablespoons butter

4 packages (16 ounces each) frozen sliced peaches, thawed and drained

1 cup fresh blueberries

½ cup packed brown sugar

¼ cup all-purpose flour

½ teaspoon vanilla

¼ teaspoon ground nutmeg

1¼ cups biscuit baking mix

⅓ cup milk

2 tablespoons butter, melted

2 tablespoons granulated sugar

1. Preheat oven to 375°F.

2. Melt 3 tablespoons butter in large skillet (not nonstick) over medium heat. Cook and stir 3 minutes or until butter has nutty aroma and turns light brown in color. Add peaches; cook and stir 2 minutes.

3. Combine peaches, blueberries, brown sugar, flour, vanilla and nutmeg in large bowl; toss to coat. Spoon into 2-quart oval baking dish.

4. Bake 10 minutes. Meanwhile, combine baking mix, milk, 2 tablespoons melted butter and granulated sugar in medium bowl; mix well. Drop 8 equal spoonfuls of batter over warm fruit mixture.

5. Bake 30 to 35 minutes or until biscuits are deep golden brown and cooked on bottom. Cool 10 minutes. Serve warm.

CRANBERRY PUMPKIN NUT BREAD

Makes 1 loaf

2 cups all-purpose flour

2 teaspoons pumpkin pie spice

1 teaspoon baking powder

½ teaspoon baking soda

½ teaspoon salt

1 cup canned pumpkin

¾ cup granulated sugar

½ cup packed brown sugar

2 eggs

⅓ cup vegetable or canola oil

1 cup chopped dried cranberries

¾ cup chopped macadamia nuts, toasted*

To toast macadamia nuts, spread on baking sheet. Bake in 350°F oven 8 to 10 minutes or until lightly browned, stirring occasionally.

1. Preheat oven to 350°F. Spray 9×5-inch loaf pan with nonstick cooking spray.

2. Combine flour, pumpkin pie spice, baking powder, baking soda and salt in large bowl; mix well. Combine pumpkin, granulated sugar, brown sugar, eggs and oil in medium bowl; stir until well blended. Add to flour mixture; stir just until dry ingredients are moistened. Stir in cranberries and nuts. Pour batter into prepared pan.

3. Bake 45 to 50 minutes or until toothpick inserted into center comes out clean. Cool in pan 15 minutes; remove to wire rack to cool completely.

Sweet Potato Pecan Pie

Makes 8 servings

- 1 sweet potato (about 1 pound)
- 3 eggs, divided
- 8 tablespoons granulated sugar, divided
- 8 tablespoons packed brown sugar, divided
- 2 tablespoons butter, melted, divided
- ½ teaspoon ground cinnamon
- ½ teaspoon salt, divided
- 1 frozen 9-inch deep-dish pie crust
- ½ cup dark corn syrup
- 1½ teaspoons vanilla
- 1½ teaspoons lemon juice
- 1 cup pecan halves
- Vanilla ice cream (optional)

1. Preheat oven to 350°F. Prick sweet potato all over with fork. Bake 1 hour or until fork-tender; let stand until cool enough to handle. Peel sweet potato; place in bowl of electric stand mixer. *Reduce oven temperature to 300°F.*

2. Add 1 egg, 2 tablespoons granulated sugar, 2 tablespoons brown sugar, 1 tablespoon butter, cinnamon and ¼ teaspoon salt to bowl with sweet potato; beat at medium speed 5 minutes or until smooth and fluffy. Spread mixture in frozen crust; place in refrigerator.

3. Combine corn syrup, remaining 6 tablespoons granulated sugar, 6 tablespoons brown sugar, 1 tablespoon butter, vanilla, lemon juice and remaining ¼ teaspoon salt in clean mixer bowl; beat at medium speed 5 minutes. Add remaining 2 eggs; beat 5 minutes. Place crust on baking sheet. Spread pecans over sweet potato filling; pour corn syrup mixture evenly over pecans.

4. Bake 1 hour or until center is set and top is deep golden brown. Cool completely. Serve with ice cream, if desired.

Nutty Chocolate Oat Bars

Makes 2 to 3 dozen bars

1 cup all-purpose flour

1 cup old-fashioned oats

¾ cup packed brown sugar

½ cup (1 stick) butter, softened

1 can (14 ounces) sweetened condensed milk

1 cup chopped walnuts or pecans

1 cup semisweet chocolate chips

1. Preheat oven to 350°F. Combine flour, oats, brown sugar and butter in large bowl; stir until crumbly.

2. Reserve ½ cup oat mixture for topping. Press remaining mixture firmly on bottom of ungreased 13×9-inch baking pan.

3. Bake 10 minutes. Remove from oven; pour condensed milk evenly over crust. Sprinkle with walnuts and chocolate chips. Top with reserved oat mixture; press down firmly.

4. Bake 25 minutes or until top is lightly browned. Cool completely in pan on wire rack. Cut into bars.

WARM MIXED BERRY PIE

Makes 8 servings

2 packages (12 ounces each) frozen mixed berries

⅓ cup sugar

3 tablespoons cornstarch

2 teaspoons grated orange peel

¼ teaspoon ground ginger

1 refrigerated pie crust (half of 15-ounce package)

1. Preheat oven to 350°F.

2. Combine berries, sugar, cornstarch, orange peel and ginger in large bowl; toss gently to coat. Spoon into large cast iron skillet.

3. Roll out pie crust into 12-inch circle. Place over fruit; flute edge as desired. Cut several slits in pie crust to allow steam to escape.

4. Bake 1 hour or until crust is golden brown. Let stand 1 hour before slicing.

Chocolate Banana Peanut Butter Poke Cake

Makes 12 to 15 servings

1 package (about 15 ounces) chocolate cake mix, plus ingredients to prepare mix

½ cup (1 stick) butter, softened

½ cup peanut butter (not natural)

4 to 5 teaspoons milk

1 to 2 cups powdered sugar

1 package (4-serving size) banana cream instant pudding and pie filling mix, plus ingredients to prepare mix

1. Prepare and bake cake mix according to package directions for 13×9-inch pan. Cool completely in pan on wire rack.

2. Beat butter in large bowl with electric mixer at medium speed until light and fluffy. Add peanut butter and milk; beat 2 minutes or until fluffy. Gradually beat in powdered sugar, ¼ cup at a time, until frosting reaches spreadable consistency. Set aside.

3. Poke holes in cake at ½-inch intervals with wooden skewer. Prepare pudding mix according to package directions. Pour pudding over cake; top with peanut butter frosting. Refrigerate 2 to 3 hours or until firm.

CRANBERRY WALNUT GRANOLA BARS

Makes 12 bars

2 packages (3 ounces each) ramen noodles, any flavor, broken into small pieces*

¾ cup all-purpose flour

1 teaspoon pumpkin pie spice

½ teaspoon baking soda

½ teaspoon salt

1 cup packed brown sugar

¼ cup (½ stick) butter, softened

2 eggs

¼ cup orange juice

1 cup chopped walnuts

½ cup dried cranberries

Discard seasoning packets.

1. Preheat oven to 350°F. Spray 9-inch square baking pan with nonstick cooking spray.

2. Combine noodles, flour, pumpkin pie spice, baking soda and salt in medium bowl; mix well.

3. Beat brown sugar and butter in large bowl with electric mixer at medium speed until light and fluffy. Add eggs and orange juice; beat until blended. Gradually add noodle mixture; beat just until blended. Stir in walnuts and cranberries. Spread batter in prepared pan.

4. Bake 20 to 25 minutes or until toothpick inserted into center comes out clean. Cool completely before cutting into bars.

CHOCOLATE CHUNK PIZZA COOKIE

Makes 3 pizza cookies (2 to 3 servings each)

2 cups all-purpose flour

1 teaspoon baking soda

1 teaspoon salt

¾ cup (1½ sticks) butter, softened

1 cup packed brown sugar

¼ cup granulated sugar

2 eggs

1 teaspoon vanilla

1 package (about 11 ounces) chocolate chunks

Vanilla ice cream

1. Preheat oven to 400°F. Spray three 6-inch cast iron skillets, cake pans or deep-dish pizza pans with nonstick cooking spray.*

2. Combine flour, baking soda and salt in medium bowl; mix well. Beat butter, brown sugar and granulated sugar in large bowl with electric mixer at medium speed until creamy. Beat in eggs and vanilla until well blended. Gradually beat in flour mixture at low speed just until blended. Stir in chocolate chunks. Spread dough evenly in prepared pans.

3. Bake about 15 minutes or until top and edges are deep golden brown but center is still slightly soft. Top with ice cream. Serve warm.

If you don't have three skillets or pans, you can bake one cookie at a time. Refrigerate the dough between batches and make sure the skillet is completely cool before adding more dough. (Clean and spray the skillet again before adding each new batch.)

LEMON BLACKBERRY COBBLER

Makes 8 servings

1 package (about 17 ounces) sugar cookie mix

6 tablespoons (¾ stick) butter, softened

1 egg

2 tablespoons all-purpose flour, plus additional for work surface

2 tablespoons grated lemon peel

4 containers (6 ounces each) fresh blackberries

⅓ cup sugar

3 tablespoons lemon juice

3 tablespoons cornstarch

1. Preheat oven to 375°F.

2. Combine sugar cookie mix, butter, egg and 2 tablespoons flour in large bowl; mix well. Divide dough in half; wrap and reserve half for another use. Add lemon peel to remaining dough. Wrap with plastic wrap; refrigerate 30 minutes or until firm.

3. Combine blackberries, sugar, lemon juice and cornstarch in medium bowl; toss gently to coat. Spoon into 9-inch deep-dish pie plate.

4. Roll out dough into 9-inch circle on lightly floured surface; cut into 12 equal strips. Arrange strips in lattice design over blackberries; trim excess dough from edge. (If dough becomes too soft to work with, refrigerate again before doing lattice.)

5. Bake 30 minutes. *Reduce oven temperature to 325°F.* Cover edge of crust with foil if overbrowning. Bake 18 to 20 minutes or until toothpick inserted into center of crust comes out clean. Let stand at least 15 minutes before serving.

Pumpkin Swirl Brownies

Makes about 16 servings

Pumpkin Swirl

- 4 ounces cream cheese, softened
- ½ cup canned pumpkin
- 1 egg
- 3 tablespoons sugar
- ¾ teaspoon pumpkin pie spice
- Pinch salt

Brownies

- ½ cup (1 stick) butter
- 6 ounces semisweet chocolate, chopped
- 1 cup sugar
- 3 eggs
- 1 teaspoon vanilla
- ¾ cup all-purpose flour
- 2 tablespoons unsweetened cocoa powder
- ½ teaspoon salt

1. Preheat oven to 350°F. Spray 8-inch square baking pan with nonstick cooking spray or line with parchment paper.

2. Combine cream cheese, pumpkin, 1 egg, 3 tablespoons sugar, pumpkin pie spice and pinch of salt in medium bowl; beat until smooth.

3. Melt butter and chocolate in medium saucepan over low heat, stirring frequently. Remove from heat; stir in 1 cup sugar until blended. Beat in eggs, one at a time, until well blended. Stir in vanilla. Add flour, cocoa and ½ teaspoon salt; stir until blended. Reserve ⅓ cup brownie batter; spread remaining batter in prepared pan.

4. Spread pumpkin mixture evenly over brownie batter. Drop reserved brownie batter by teaspoonfuls over pumpkin layer; draw tip of knife through top of both batters to marbleize. (If reserved brownie batter has become very thick upon standing, microwave on LOW (30%) 20 to 30 seconds or until loosened, stirring at 10-second intervals.)

5. Bake 28 to 30 minutes or just until center is set and edges begin to pull away from sides of pan. (Toothpick will come out with fudgy crumbs.) Cool in pan on wire rack.

CARROT CAKE

Makes 8 to 10 servings

CAKE

- 2 cups all-purpose flour
- 2 teaspoons baking soda
- 2 teaspoons ground cinnamon
- 1 teaspoon salt
- 4 eggs
- 2¼ cups granulated sugar
- 1 cup vegetable oil
- 1 cup buttermilk
- 1 tablespoon vanilla
- 3 medium carrots, shredded (3 cups)
- 3 cups walnuts, chopped and toasted, divided
- 1 cup shredded coconut
- 1 can (8 ounces) crushed pineapple

FROSTING

- 2 packages (8 ounces each) cream cheese, softened
- 1 cup (2 sticks) butter, softened
- Pinch salt
- 3 cups powdered sugar
- 1 tablespoon orange juice
- 2 teaspoons grated orange peel
- 1 teaspoon vanilla

1. Preheat oven to 350°F. Spray two 9-inch round cake pans with nonstick cooking spray. Line bottoms of pans with parchment paper; spray with cooking spray.

2. Combine flour, baking soda, cinnamon and 1 teaspoon salt in medium bowl; mix well. Whisk eggs in large bowl until blended. Add granulated sugar, oil, buttermilk and 1 tablespoon vanilla; whisk until well blended. Add flour mixture; stir until blended. Add carrots, 1 cup walnuts, coconut and pineapple; stir just until blended. Pour batter into prepared pans.

3. Bake 25 to 30 minutes or until toothpick inserted into centers comes out clean. Cool in pans 10 minutes; remove to wire racks to cool completely.

4. Beat cream cheese, butter and pinch of salt in large bowl with electric mixer at medium speed 3 minutes or until creamy. Add powdered sugar, orange juice, orange peel and 1 teaspoon vanilla; beat at low speed until blended. Beat at medium speed 2 minutes or until frosting is smooth.

5. Place one cake layer on serving plate; spread with 2 cups frosting. Top with second cake layer; frost top and side of cake with remaining frosting. Press 1¾ cups walnuts onto side of cake. Sprinkle remaining ¼ cup walnuts over top of cake.

PLUM RHUBARB CRUMBLE

Makes 6 to 8 servings

1½ pounds plums, each pitted and cut into 8 wedges (4 cups)

1½ pounds rhubarb, cut into ½-inch pieces (5 cups)

1 cup granulated sugar

1 teaspoon finely grated fresh ginger

¼ teaspoon ground nutmeg

3 tablespoons cornstarch

¾ cup old-fashioned oats

½ cup all-purpose flour

½ cup packed brown sugar

½ cup sliced almonds, toasted*

¼ teaspoon salt

½ cup (1 stick) cold butter, cut into small pieces

*To toast almonds, spread on ungreased baking sheet. Bake in preheated 350°F oven 5 minutes or until golden brown, stirring frequently.

1. Combine plums, rhubarb, granulated sugar, ginger and nutmeg in large bowl; toss to coat. Cover and let stand at room temperature 2 hours.

2. Preheat oven to 375°F. Spray 9-inch round or square baking dish with nonstick cooking spray. Line baking sheet with foil.

3. Pour juices from fruit mixture into small saucepan; bring to a boil over medium-high heat. Cook about 12 minutes or until reduced to syrupy consistency, stirring occasionally. Stir in cornstarch until well blended. Stir mixture into bowl with fruit; pour into prepared baking dish.

4. Combine oats, flour, brown sugar, almonds and salt in medium bowl; mix well. Add butter; mix with fingertips until butter is evenly distributed and mixture is clumpy. Sprinkle evenly over fruit mixture. Place baking dish on prepared baking sheet.

5. Bake about 50 minutes or until filling is bubbly and topping is golden brown. Cool 1 hour before serving.

INDEX

METRIC CONVERSION CHART

VOLUME MEASUREMENTS (dry)

$^1/_8$ teaspoon = 0.5 mL
$^1/_4$ teaspoon = 1 mL
$^1/_2$ teaspoon = 2 mL
$^3/_4$ teaspoon = 4 mL
1 teaspoon = 5 mL
1 tablespoon = 15 mL
2 tablespoons = 30 mL
$^1/_4$ cup = 60 mL
$^1/_3$ cup = 75 mL
$^1/_2$ cup = 125 mL
$^2/_3$ cup = 150 mL
$^3/_4$ cup = 175 mL
1 cup = 250 mL
2 cups = 1 pint = 500 mL
3 cups = 750 mL
4 cups = 1 quart = 1 L

VOLUME MEASUREMENTS (fluid)

1 fluid ounce (2 tablespoons) = 30 mL
4 fluid ounces ($^1/_2$ cup) = 125 mL
8 fluid ounces (1 cup) = 250 mL
12 fluid ounces (1$^1/_2$ cups) = 375 mL
16 fluid ounces (2 cups) = 500 mL

WEIGHTS (mass)

$^1/_2$ ounce = 15 g
1 ounce = 30 g
3 ounces = 90 g
4 ounces = 120 g
8 ounces = 225 g
10 ounces = 285 g
12 ounces = 360 g
16 ounces = 1 pound = 450 g

DIMENSIONS

$^1/_{16}$ inch = 2 mm
$^1/_8$ inch = 3 mm
$^1/_4$ inch = 6 mm
$^1/_2$ inch = 1.5 cm
$^3/_4$ inch = 2 cm
1 inch = 2.5 cm

OVEN TEMPERATURES

250°F = 120°C
275°F = 140°C
300°F = 150°C
325°F = 160°C
350°F = 180°C
375°F = 190°C
400°F = 200°C
425°F = 220°C
450°F = 230°C

BAKING PAN SIZES

Utensil	Size in Inches/Quarts	Metric Volume	Size in Centimeters
Baking or Cake Pan (square or rectangular)	8×8×2	2 L	20×20×5
	9×9×2	2.5 L	23×23×5
	12×8×2	3 L	30×20×5
	13×9×2	3.5 L	33×23×5
Loaf Pan	8×4×3	1.5 L	20×10×7
	9×5×3	2 L	23×13×7
Round Layer Cake Pan	8×1½	1.2 L	20×4
	9×1½	1.5 L	23×4
Pie Plate	8×1¼	750 mL	20×3
	9×1¼	1 L	23×3
Baking Dish or Casserole	1 quart	1 L	—
	1½ quart	1.5 L	—
	2 quart	2 L	—